The
REAL RULES

HOW TO FIND
THE *RIGHT* MAN
FOR THE *REAL* YOU

Barbara De Angelis, Ph.D.

A DELL BOOK

Published by
Dell Publishing
a division of
Bantam Doubleday Dell Publishing Group, Inc.
1540 Broadway
New York, New York 10036

ISBN: 0-440-22448-9

Printed in the United States of America

Published simultaneously in Canada

March 1997

10   9   8   7   6   5   4   3   2   1

OPM

"Don't talk to a man first . . ."? "Let him take the lead . . ."? "Be quiet and reserved . . ."?
**THE ONLY THING "THE RULES"
WILL GET YOU IS THE *WRONG* MAN.
LET THE REAL RULES
HELP YOU FIND THE *RIGHT* ONE.**

If you think that playing games with a man will make him a loving, sharing partner, think again! Anyone who advises: "Don't meet him halfway," "Rarely return his calls," and "If you don't get jewelry . . . you might as well call it quits" doesn't know the first thing about relationships and true commitment. The old rules our grandmothers followed to get a man don't work today (and, in fact, they never did). They were part of the same package that kept women from voicing their opinions, having careers, and earning equal wages.

As the #1 *New York Times* bestselling author of six classic books on love, and with nearly two decades of experience helping couples achieve fulfilling, committed relationships, Barbara De Angelis, Ph.D., knows that scheming and manipulation don't work. Her remarkable formula for finding a relationship based on honesty and love replaces the old rules with *The Real Rules*—real advice that will help you find the *right* partner and create a marriage that will last a lifetime.

*ADVICE IS ONLY AS GOOD AS THE PERSON
WHO OFFERS IT. ISN'T IT TIME TO LISTEN TO
SOMEONE WHO REALLY KNOWS . . .*
**BARBARA DE ANGELIS, Ph.D.
THE REAL RULES**

Also by Barbara De Angelis

ASK BARBARA

REAL MOMENTS® FOR LOVERS

REAL MOMENTS®

ARE YOU THE ONE FOR ME?

SECRETS ABOUT MEN EVERY WOMAN SHOULD KNOW

HOW TO MAKE LOVE ALL THE TIME

THE REAL RULES

Part 3
THE REAL RULES FOR COMMUNICATING WITH MEN

Part 4
THE REAL RULES ABOUT SEX

Part 5
THE REAL RULES ABOUT GETTING A MAN TO MAKE A COMMITMENT

Part 6
HOW TO LIVE YOUR LIFE WITH THE REAL RULES

FOREWORD

Let me tell you the story of how I decided to write *The Real Rules:*

One day in the fall of 1996, I was having lunch with several female friends. As we started on our salads, one of the women asked: "So Barbara, what do you think of that book everyone's talking about—*The Rules?*" Now, I'd heard about this book which supposedly tells women how to get a man to marry them, but hadn't actually seen it, so I answered frankly, "I haven't read it."

"You haven't?" She reached into her purse and handed me a small paperback. "Here—someone in my office just gave me this as a joke. You aren't going to believe this book!"

Now I was intrigued. Naturally, over the years, as a leading authority on relationships, I've always been asked my opinion about other books on love, but even when I've disagreed with the author's thinking, I have never publicly criticized what I've read—that's just not my style. And so I was completely unprepared for what happened next.

I looked at the book: *The Rules.* The cover looked harmless enough. Then, I opened the book and began to read—one piece of bad, recycled, antiquated advice after another—the kind of advice my grandmother gave my mother at the same time that she informed her she could get pregnant from kissing a man. At first, I thought that I'd misunderstood, that maybe this was one of those comic takeoffs on self-help books. Then, to my horror, as each chapter got progressively worse, I realized that this wasn't a joke—*this was supposed to be serious!*

I could hardly believe what I was reading:

". . . the man must take the lead . . ."

". . . be quiet and mysterious, act ladylike . . ."

". . . don't say much, let him do all the thinking, the talking . . ."

". . . he runs the show . . ."

". . . if you don't get jewelry . . . you might as well call it quits . . ."

". . . try wearing tight jeans, a miniskirt, or a deep V-necked shirt . . ."

". . . if you have a bad nose, get a nose job."

". . . overweight is not *The Rules* . . ."

These weren't the rules for happiness—they were the rules for messing up your love life and behaving like the worst stereotype of a superficial, submissive woman!!

What I'm talking about goes way beyond any current book—it goes back centuries. They are the very ideas that caused millions of women (including me) to get into bad relationships with men they shouldn't have even dated in the first place; the very ideas that had trapped so many women into love-starved, meaningless marriages they were afraid to leave; the very ideas that had created whole generations of women with low self-esteem; the very ideas from which I and so many other successful and happy women had spent our whole lives working hard to break free.

I thought about all the unsuspecting women who were desperately putting *The Rules* into practice, not realizing the price they were eventually going to pay for compromising their honesty, integrity, and self-respect in order to trap a man.

I thought about all the teenage girls reading this junk, believing it was the truth, and getting their first boyfriend by playing games, showing their cleavage, and keeping their mouths shut.

I thought of the inevitable backlash from men who would hear about The Rules and conclude, *"I was right—women are just controlling, manipulative bitches."*

Suddenly, I realized that the book I was holding in my hand wasn't merely amusing, silly, or just incredibly stupid—**it was wrong**. It went against everything I've taught for the past twenty years, and everything I know to be healthy in relationships.

That's when I knew I had to write **The Real Rules**. . . .

• • •

I dedicate *The Real Rules* to every woman who has ever had her heart broken by falling in love with a man who wasn't good for her.

I dedicate *The Real Rules* to every woman who has ever believed she needs to become a man's perfect-bodied, plastic fantasy in order to get his love.

I dedicate *The Real Rules* to every woman who has ever been afraid to share her real feelings, desires, or concerns with a man for fear that he'll tell her she's too "needy and demanding."

I dedicate *The Real Rules* to every woman who has ever been so afraid of losing a man that she sacrificed her opinions, her values, and her self-respect.

I dedicate *The Real Rules* to every woman who has ever lost herself so deeply in trying to please a man that she doesn't know who *she* is anymore.

I dedicate *The Real Rules* to every mother who doesn't want her daughter to make the same mistakes in love that she did, and every daughter who doesn't want to end up like her mother.

I dedicate *The Real Rules* to every woman who dreams of having a relationship with a *real* man based on *real* equality—no games, no power struggles, just a loving, intimate, mutually respectful partnership.

And I dedicate *The Real Rules* to every *real* man out there who wants a *real* woman—*a woman you can trust and respect who has an honest mind and a loving heart.*

I offer this with love, from me to you.
The Real Truth.
The Real Rules . . .

Barbara De Angelis

Part 1

THE REAL RULES: WHAT THEY ARE AND WHY YOU NEED THEM

WHAT ARE THE REAL RULES?

When I was a little girl, I believed that the happiest day of my life would be my wedding day. Even though I knew nothing about relationships, I already understood that the day I married the man of my dreams would signify a great accomplishment in my life, as it did in the life of all women—the day I officially captured a man. No one ever actually used the word "capture" in referring to my search for a mate. Yet the message from my family and from society was clear: I was supposed to "find" myself a husband, "get" a man," "catch" a guy.

It was also clear that in the grown-up world, women who hadn't "gotten" a man, and, even worse, had never "gotten" married, were to be pitied, like the weak animals in a herd who just couldn't catch any prey. I'd hear my relatives whisper, *"So and so's daughter is thirty-two, and she's not married. Poor thing. I wonder what's wrong with her . . ."*

And so like millions of women throughout history, I got the message: **my value as a woman lay in my ability to "get" a man.** Somehow, if I didn't get a man, I would be less of a woman. And if I was lucky enough to get a man with a prestigious job or money or both, then I would be a real winner.

It should come as no surprise, then, that by the time I was seventeen years old, my main goal in life was to be in a relationship with a guy. Looking back, I realize that it didn't actually matter *who* he was, as long as I was going steady. Did I ever ask myself if I was really happy? Did I ask myself if he respected me and supported my goals? Did I ask myself if he was everything I was looking for in a boyfriend? Of course not. I just wanted to be part of a couple. *I was less concerned with who I was with, than the fact that I was with* **someone.**

Eventually, I went off to college, and this pattern continued. Someone would indicate that he liked me, would chase after me a bit, and I'd get into a relationship with him. (When I recall some of the guys I was involved with, I shudder . . . you know the feeling, right!!?) Naturally, these relationships never worked. How could they? **My goal was the acquisition of a man, not the creation of a really good relationship.** I was so busy trying to GET the guy that I never asked myself if I really wanted to be with who I ended up with.

Finally, when I was twenty-one, the big moment arrived. A young man asked me to marry him. Never mind that I wasn't really in love with him; never mind that I hardly knew anything about him; never mind that we were totally incompatible. This was what I'd been waiting for—a proposal, and so of course, I said "yes." At last—I'd be Mrs. Barbara Somebody! I'd done it . . . I'd gotten a man!!

You can imagine, then, my heartbreak when, after five brief but nightmarish months, I found myself getting the marriage annulled. "How could this have happened?" I asked myself in disbelief. "All I've ever wanted was to be married."

It took me many years and several other painful relationships to figure out the answer:

My heart was broken because I'd been following THE OLD RULE.

What was THE OLD RULE that had broken my heart? It was the unspoken but powerful message behind everything my family had taught me, behind everything I'd observed about society's treatment of women.

THE OLD RULE WAS:

THE GOAL OF A WOMAN'S LIFE IS TO FIND A MAN AND GET MARRIED.

I'd followed THE OLD RULE, and I'd gotten a man. The problem was, *I had wanted to be married, more than I wanted to be married to the* right *person.* As I said earlier: **the goal of a woman who follows THE OLD RULE is the** *acquisition* **of a man,** *not* **the creation of a healthy loving relationship.**

This is what happens when you follow THE OLD RULE to get a man. You focus your energy and your awareness on the **getting** part of the process as opposed to focusing it on **whom** you're getting. And one day, you wake up and realize you're in a rela-

tionship that's not at all what you want with someone who's not at all whom you want.

Like millions of women before me and millions of
women after me who followed THE OLD RULE and
ended up in the wrong relationship, I'd been so concerned about getting *someone* to love me that I'd
never taken the time to really ask myself if *I* loved
him. I'd been so concerned about getting a commitment from him that I'd never asked myself if he was
the kind of man *I* wanted to commit to. I'd been so
concerned about getting him to think that I was everything he wanted that I'd never asked myself if he
was everything *I* wanted.

It took me until my mid-thirties to realize that I
had been unconsciously sabotaging my love life by
following THE OLD RULE. And it was only when I
stopped practicing this old rule, and applied THE
REAL RULES that are in this book, that I finally
found the right man, created the healthy relationship
I'd always wanted, and got married—this time, for
the right reasons . . .

Where did THE OLD RULE that has dominated so
many women's lives come from? It developed based
on thousands of years of history during which
women had no equal rights or opportunities, no jobs
or ability to earn our own income, and truly needed
a man, any man, for our physical survival. We didn't
have a choice—we either got married to whomever
would have us, or entered a convent. (Having our
own apartment with a friend was not an option . . .)

Lots of things made sense centuries ago that don't make sense now—using a horse for transportation; cooking your meals over a fire; abstaining from sex because you didn't want to have any more children. Now you have other choices that make life a lot easier, and much more enjoyable. That's called progress. *The OLD RULE and all the "sub-rules" that stem from it, made sense thousands of years ago, maybe even a hundred years ago. But they don't make sense now.*

Whether you recently read about this outdated thinking in a book, heard or still hear it from family members or girlfriends, or just realize, like I did, that it's been unconsciously running and ruining your love life, one thing is true: As a woman on the threshold of the twenty-first century, you have other choices. And that's what THE REAL RULES are about.

THE REAL RULES are positive principles about love and relationships that will take you into a more powerful, more fulfilled future, rather than trapping you in a limited past.

THE REAL RULES aren't about trying to be what a man wants so he'll marry you. Instead, *THE REAL RULES are about becoming who you really are as a woman, and finding a man who loves you because of it.*

THE REAL RULES won't just teach you how to get a man—they'll teach you how to get the *right* man.

Most importantly, THE REAL RULES are NOT

based on the negative principle of FEAR—fear of being alone, fear of being unattractive, fear of a man becoming bored with you if you're not "mysterious," fear of making one wrong move or saying one wrong thing and "blowing" a whole relationship. *When your behavior or choices are motivated by fear, you're never acting from your most powerful self.*

Instead THE REAL RULES *are* based on the positive principle of LOVE—loving and honoring your own thoughts, needs, and feelings as a woman, loving and honoring your partner's own thoughts, needs, and feelings as a man, and expressing that love for yourself and for him by practicing honesty, kindness, and respect in all of your behaviors and communications.

There are 25 REAL RULES I'll be sharing with you in the following chapters. All of THE REAL RULES are based on these basic principles that I call

THE FOUR LAWS OF LOVE

#1. The purpose of your life isn't to get married. The purpose of your life is to grow into the most loving, fulfilled, *real* woman you can be.

#2. Your love life shouldn't focus on getting *a* man, but rather on finding the *right* man for the *real* you.

#3. Once you have found the *right* man, the goal shouldn't be getting him to make the ultimate commitment, but rather, creating a healthy, loving, mutually respectful *real* relationship.

#4. When you create a healthy, mutually respectful, *real* relationship with the right man, a loving commitment between you will naturally occur.

Soon I'll be presenting the specific REAL RULES, but you can start replacing OLD RULES THINKING with REAL RULES THINKING even after reading just these few pages. Here's a chart to help you:

OLD RULES THINKING	REAL RULES THINKING
I want a man	I want the *right* man for me
I want him to love me	I want him to love me for who I *really* am
I want to become just what he's been looking for	I want to make sure he's just what *I've* been looking for
I want to get him to marry me	I want to work together to create a healthy, loving, mutually respectful relationship that grows into a commitment so our marriage will last

I'm so excited to share this information with you. I know it's going to make an enormous difference in your life, just as it did in mine. You deserve to know about **THE REAL RULES!!!**

HOW TO STOP SABOTAGING YOUR LOVE LIFE WITH THE OLD RULES

Have you been tempted to try out some so-called "techniques" you recently read in a book or magazine about THE OLD RULES in hope of getting a man to fall in love with you, or getting your boyfriend to propose?

Does the advice you heard from your mother or from friends about how to "play hard to get with men" ever run through your mind, and do you find yourself wondering if it might work for you?

Are you embarrassed to admit that, even though you disagree with them, you've secretly considered using some of THE OLD RULES because you're so tired of being single?

If you answered "yes," "maybe," or even "I'm not sure": **STOP EVERYTHING AND READ THIS CHAPTER NOW!!** Before you go out on your next date, before you talk to a man on the phone, or before you even leave the house, think about this:

- *Practicing THE OLD RULES can sabotage your self-esteem and take away your real power in relationships.*
- *Practicing THE REAL RULES, you'll not only find*

the right man for you, but you'll also feel more self-confident than ever before in all areas of your life.

Most women I know don't just want a great relationship—whether they're seventeen or seventy, they also want to feel fulfilled and powerful in their life. All of us would like to make our dreams come true, whether those dreams are to create a happy marriage and loving family, or to have our own, successful business. The dictionary defines the word "powerful" as meaning *strong, capable, confident, effective, and impressive,* versus feeling powerless—helpless, weak, ineffective, and dependent. Along with feeling powerful, most of us want to feel good about ourselves—*we want a strong sense of confidence and self-esteem.* And naturally, the more self-esteem you possess, the more capable and powerful you feel, and the more you attract the right people in life.

Well, guess what: every time you put one of the OLD RULES into practice, you are sabotaging your self-esteem and power. THE OLD RULES may seem like a silly, harmless method for getting a husband, but they're actually much more dangerous than that, because each time you act on an OLD RULE, you're reinforcing negative beliefs about yourself.

Is This the Kind of Woman You Want to Become?

The premise of THE OLD RULES is that your purpose is to find a man and get him to marry you. You are the hunter, and he is the prey. Your goal is to *catch* him. But THE OLD RULES say that a man won't naturally want to make a commitment to you—he doesn't want to be caught—so somehow, you have to trick him into it:

- You can't reveal too much about who you are, or he'll get turned off.
- You can't show your true feelings, or he'll lose interest.
- You can't be too honest, or he'll become bored with you.
- You have to look unattainable. Then, because he thinks he can't have you, he'll want you, and you've got him!!!!

This is what THE OLD RULES are all about—**methods for getting what you want from a man by being covert, dishonest, and withholding love.** There's a word for this kind of behavior:

Manipulation

Manipulation is the opposite of true power. When you are a powerful woman, you don't have to manipulate someone in order to get what you want. You don't have to pretend, play games, hide the truth, or put on an act.

This brings us to the second premise of THE OLD RULES—that you need to figure out what a particular man wants in a woman and become that so you are "easy to be with." Your goal is to fit into his picture of his ideal woman. You don't want him to have an excuse to reject you, so you act the way you think he wants you to act: Another word for this demeaning behavior is:

Masquerade

Masquerade is the opposite of true self-esteem and self-confidence. When you truly love and respect yourself, you don't have to hide parts of your personality from a man so he won't be "scared off." You don't have to lie about your feelings by acting mysterious, or bury your beliefs and opinions beneath a demure smile as you sweetly say, "Whatever *you* want is fine with me."

So each time you choose to follow an OLD RULE, you are reinforcing feelings of powerlessness, of low self-esteem: It's as if you are saying:

"I'm not smart enough, wonderful enough, or in-

teresting enough to get a man to want to spend his life with me just by being me, so I am going to have to manipulate him into wanting me, and masquerade as someone I'm not."

How the Old Rules Are the Enemy of Your Self-Esteem

Here's why the Two "M's," *Manipulation* and *Masquerade*, are the enemies of true power and self-esteem and why THE OLD RULES don't work:

1. *You never develop true* **confidence** *when you use Manipulation and Masquerade on men.* Since you know you got the guy's interest or love based on NOT behaving naturally, and NOT being yourself, you'll never feel relaxed, or trust his love for you.

2. *You never develop true* **power** *when you use Manipulation and Masquerade on men.* Since you know you used artificial techniques to get a man interested in you, you are DEPENDENT on those techniques to keep him. You can never feel truly powerful when you're DEPENDENT on something outside yourself.

3. *There is a secret formula all men recognize hidden in THE OLD RULES:*

$$M + M = B$$

This stands for:
Manipulation + Masquerade = BITCH

That's right, the B word. There's no other way to say it. It's a slang term, but we all know what it means.

Try this experiment: Ask any man to read the following description of a woman, and summarize her in *one word:*

A woman who plays games, acts hard to get, pretends she's not interested, wants you to be vulnerable and open, but won't be vulnerable and open with you, acts like she doesn't need you, judges you by the gifts you give her, makes you pay for everything, and is inconsiderate of your schedule.

I'll bet you that nine out of ten men say: **"That's easy—she's a *bitch!*"**

It's that simple. We can make it sound nicer with more intellectual words, but the bottom line is still the same—**following THE OLD RULES, no matter how good your intentions might be, will most likely make you appear to be a bitch to men. The only men who would find that kind of woman appealing are men you definitely *don't* want in your life.**

What's the alternative?
THE REAL RULES!!

Part 2

THE REAL RULES
FOR FINDING THE
RIGHT RELATIONSHIP

REAL RULE #1:
Treat Men the Way You Want Them to Treat You

REAL RULE #1 is the heart of all THE REAL RULES. It's not just about love, but about life. Does it sound familiar? It should. Maybe you learned a version of it in Bible class when you were little, or heard it preached at your church or synagogue. Traditionally it's called The Golden Rule: *Do Unto Others as You Would Have Them Do Unto You.* In India, it's called the law of karma: Your good actions toward others will eventually and inevitably produce good effects in your own life; your bad actions toward others will produce undesirable effects in your own life. Or, as we say in America:

> *"What goes around comes around."*

However you word it, REAL RULE #1 means the same thing: Treat people (in this case men) the way you would like them to treat you.

- If you want a man to be considerate to you, be considerate to him.

- If you want a man to be honest with you, be honest with him.

- If you want a man to be respectful of you, be respectful of him.
- If you want a man to open up to you, open up to him.

Of course, the flip side of REAL RULE #1 is: DON'T TREAT A MAN THE WAY YOU DON'T WANT HIM TO TREAT YOU.

- If you don't want a man to play games with you, don't play games with him.
- If you don't want a man to manipulate you, don't manipulate him.
- If you don't want a man to be cold to you, don't be cold to him.
- If you don't want a man to share who he really is with you, don't share who you really are with him . . . Get the point . . . ?

REAL RULE #1 is based on the belief that, from a cosmic or spiritual point of view, all beings are created equal and have equal value—men aren't more valuable or superior to women, and women aren't more valuable or superior to men. Therefore, men should be treated with the same courtesy and respect you'd like them to show you. It's common sense.

If you're a woman who wants equal pay for your work, equal rights in society, and equal opportunities in your life, how can you offer men anything less than equality in a relationship? *You can't have it both ways.* You can't say "I think my boyfriend and I are equal, but I think he should bear the burden of making all the moves in the relationship and be the only one who faces rejection." That's just plain selfish, and it's not playing by THE REAL RULES.

Even if you forget all of the other REAL RULES, when in doubt, go back to REAL RULE #1, and you'll probably make the right decision about how to act or what to say in a relationship. That's because your decision will be based on respect and fairness.

What about the OLD RULES idea that the natural order of life is for men to pursue women, that men are like animals that love the chase, and that we have to treat them as such, making ourselves unavailable, making it impossible for them to know how we are feeling? This is disrespectful, demeaning garbage. Saying men love to fight and go to war because they love a challenge, and therefore, you should make his conquest of you as difficult as possible is just as stupid as saying that women love to clean toilets and scrub floors, and that it's the natural order of things for us to be second-class citizens. Yes, it is true that men have been *conditioned* throughout history to play the role of the hunter, but that doesn't mean you have to indulge them in it now by acting like fleeing prey! Why bring out the worst in a man on purpose?

How would you like it if your boss told you he was never going to promote you because you were a woman, and just weren't as capable as men? How would you like it if you were trying to get a scholarship to attend graduate school and your advisor gave the scholarship to a guy, claiming that women weren't as smart as men? You'd be outraged, wouldn't you? Is that attitude any worse than thinking men should be treated with different rules in relationships than apply to you?

REAL RULE #1 says that the simple test for any rule you're thinking of using as a guideline in a relationship is this: *REVERSE IT*, making it the man's rule about his treatment of you, and see if it still seems fair.

For instance, an OLD RULE is: *"Don't Call Him and Rarely Return His Calls."* Now, reverse it, and imagine it's his rule: *"Don't Call Her and Rarely Return Her Calls."* Does this sound like the kind of guy you'd want to get involved with? I don't think so . . .

Let's try another one: *"Don't Talk to a Man First."* Okay, switch it: *"Don't Talk to a Woman First."* Imagine how thrilling your love life would be if you walked into a party, and knew that all the men were following this rule, and you were going to have to make every move if you even wanted to have a conversation.

I think you get my point. REAL RULE #1 reminds you that for a rule to be valid, it has to be fair. *If, on the other hand, you, like many OLD RULES women, have one set of rules for how you get to treat a man, but another set of rules for how he has to treat you, you're cheating.*

So when in doubt, refer to REAL RULE #1. For example, a friend just gave you two tickets to a hot concert, and you're wondering whether to invite a guy you've just started dating. Use the REAL RULE: Would you have liked it if he invited you to a concert? Yes? Well, then go for it. Or let's say you're on a date with a man you really like, and you're having a great time. Should you say anything? Use the REAL RULE: Would you like it if he told you he was having a good time? Yes? So go ahead.

What's the worst thing that can happen in these situations? You exhibit some kindness, some caring, some enthusiasm, and it isn't returned . . . **SO WHAT!!!!** Even if the relationship goes nowhere, you didn't lose anything. Whenever you share your goodness, your passion for life, and your heart, you always end up winning, because what you put out into the Universe *will* come back to you.

REAL RULE #2:
Remember That Men Need as Much Love and Reassurance as You Do

Before we start getting into the more specific REAL RULES, you need to understand REAL RULE #2. This REAL RULE is not so much a behavior as *an attitude you have about men* when you follow THE REAL RULES. Most important, it's an *attitude that you should carry with you into all of your interactions with men.* Men will pick up on this attitude, conclude that you understand them, and be much more apt to open their hearts to you.

I've spent over twenty years of my life studying men, giving seminars to men, answering thousands of letters from men, talking to women about men and to men about themselves. I'm here to tell you that, contrary to popular belief, *men are just as sensitive as women, and need just as much love and reassurance as we do.* This is REAL RULE #2. Every man you'll ever meet will fall into one of three categories:

Category One—Men you don't want. There are men who have serious problems in the areas of commitment, intimacy, and integrity. They're just not ready for a relationship with anyone. These poor guys need a lot of work, though they would probably disagree with that assessment! By the way, these are usually the very men who respond to OLD RULES chase games. (See REAL RULE #3)

Category Two—Perfect, enlightened men with no emotional baggage, no insecurities, and fully developed psychic abilities which allow them to know and fulfill your needs at all times. Needless to say, there is no one in this category, except for a handful of swamis, priests, and monks, and they aren't available.

Category Three—Men who want a loving, committed relationship, but just like you, are secretly scared of rejection, afraid of getting hurt, and therefore, need love and encouragement.

It should be obvious that Category One Men are to be avoided like the plague (See REAL RULES #8–13). Category Two men aren't an option! That means the majority of the men you'll meet will belong to Category Three.

Here's the secret truth about Category Three men: they're not that different from you or any other woman in one significant way—*they feel as deeply, and again, they need as much love and reassurance as you do.* They may not admit this up front; they may not even admit it after you're married. But believe me, it's true. In their hearts, men need to feel loved, to feel special, to feel safe, and to feel they are doing a good job in life and in relationships.

You know how your mind fills you with all kinds of fears when you're considering letting a man know you're interested? Men feel the same way when they're considering approaching you. You know how nervous you feel before a date with a new guy you really like? Men feel the same way before a date with you. In fact, they feel worse, because according to the OLD RULES, it's the man's responsibility to make the first move, request the date, make the plans, reach out for affection, all the way down the line to proposing marriage. Think about it—*one situation after another where he's setting himself up for potential rejection.*

Here's a chart to help you understand more about REAL RULE #2:

MEN'S SECRET DESIRES	MEN'S SECRET FEARS
Wants to make you happy.	Fear he doesn't know how.
Wants to please you.	Fear he won't be enough.
Wants to do things right.	Fear he'll make a mistake.
Wants to open up and love.	Fear that you'll reject him.

Let me ask you a question: *When do you feel safe to really open up?* For most women, the answer is: "When I feel really loved." Guess what . . . the same REAL RULE is true for men. **The more you love and appreciate a good man, the safer he's going to feel, and the more he'll open up to loving you.**

Applying Real Rule #2 means never forgetting

that inside of every incredibly desirable man you're dying to get close to is a scared little boy who has the same fear of rejection that you have. Don't underestimate the power you have to hurt him, whether by acting cold, poking fun at something he said, or making a sarcastic remark about something he didn't do well. He may never talk about it, but believe me, he'll remember it.

So instead of walking around feeling so intimidated by men, start to practice looking at them with different, more sensitive eyes, recognizing that they need your love just as much as you need theirs. You'll feel a lot more relaxed and spontaneous around men when you remember REAL RULE #2. Believe me, the more you show a guy that you're not stereotyping him as a "typical," shut down, emotionally backward male, the sooner he'll open up and reach out to make you a part of his life.

REAL RULE #3:
Stay Away From Men Who Don't Like THE REAL RULES

What's one of the biggest problems you have in the beginning of any relationship?—*How to tell whether or not you're with the wrong man before things get too serious.* How many times have you gotten involved with a guy, maybe even slept with him, only to find out three or six or nine months later that he was not the kind of person you wanted to be with, and that in fact, you didn't even like or respect him?!!!

Here's one of the greatest benefits of using THE REAL RULES—**when you put THE REAL RULES into practice, the wrong men will automatically eliminate themselves from your life.** *Why? Because THE REAL RULES will make the wrong men uncomfortable!!*

THE REAL RULES are like a "healthy man detector." Guys who are good for you will love THE REAL RULES. Guys with unhealthy love habits will hate THE REAL RULES.

Let's face it—there are some men out there who do fit the OLD RULES stereotype. They're the kind of guys that call women they hardly know "hon," "babe," and "doll." They think women should be "protected" from having too many responsibilities in life. They believe in the "boys will be boys" mentality—in other words, they expect to do what they want to without your feedback. They may act like you're their princess, but there's no doubt in their minds that they're the king.

These men will love chasing you. It makes them feel successful, potent, manly. The pursuit and capture feeds into their unfulfilled need to feel powerful. Therefore, they like women who are coy, manipulative, and withholding, because they get excited by the challenge of conquering you. When you finally submit, they've won, and in spite of the sparkling ring on your finger, you've lost. Why? *OLD RULES MEN don't want a real woman—they want a trophy, a possession, a prize.*

OLD RULES MEN:

- Want to feel like they're in control
- Think of the male sex as superior
- Believe women have a limited role in life
- Are uncomfortable with real intimacy
- Don't like powerful women
- Think their opinion counts more
- Are addicted to the chase, and are more likely to cheat when bored
- Judge you by your looks, your weight, and your breast size

- Want to feel smarter than you
- Don't like to be questioned or challenged
- Aren't interested in improving themselves for you
- Don't want the relationship to go too deep, even if you're married
- Will be threatened if you surpass them in any area (your intellect, your income, etc.)

If you're looking for this kind of husband, you might as well throw this book away right now, because OLD RULES men don't like REAL RULES WOMEN since you're not willing to play their game.

Who are these guys, and how did they get this way? They're usually men who felt overpowered as a child by a dominating father or critical mother, and decided when they grew up, they'd be the ones in control. Maybe they saw Dad treat Mom like a doormat, and decided it was either "rule or be ruled." Or maybe Dad was a passive wimp who let Mom treat him like dirt, and the child decided he'd never let a woman control *him* when he got older. The bottom line is that *OLD RULES men are always motivated by an unconscious fear of women and a secret feeling of inadequacy. After all, a really empowered, confident man doesn't have to keep proving it to himself and you every five minutes!!*

You should feel sorry for these poor misguided guys, but not enough to be with one. Don't try to rehabilitate one if you meet him, no matter how tempting it may be. Recognize him for what he is, an OLD RULES MAN, and get out of his way.

So how should you use THE REAL RULES to eliminate the wrong men and leave room for the right man? Simple—**just start putting THE REAL RULES into practice, and watch guys who are bad for you flee in the opposite direction.** For instance:

You're at a party and a friend just introduced you to a guy you find attractive. The OLD RULES say don't make eye contact, don't say much, let him take the lead, and don't act interested. Instead, try THE REAL RULES:

a) Express who you really are by talking about what interests you (REAL RULE #15)

b) Don't play games (REAL RULE #4)—if he asks you to go out with him two days from then, and you're free and want to accept, don't pretend you're busy and say "no"

c) If you like him, let him know (REAL RULE #6)—if he says he enjoyed talking with you, don't pause mysteriously and tone down your response. Tell him you also really enjoyed being with him.

Now, what if he seems turned off, or suddenly walks away during the conversation, or doesn't call you again as he said he would? Does this mean THE REAL RULES didn't work? No—quite the opposite: THEY WORKED PERFECTLY! CONGRATULATIONS! You've just used THE REAL RULES to quickly and effectively eliminate a potentially hurtful relationship with the wrong man! The sooner you spot OLD RULES guys and eliminate them as possibilities, the sooner you can find an emotionally healthy REAL RULES MAN and develop the relationship of your dreams.

REAL RULE #4:
Don't Play Games

THE REAL RULES are all about being smart. *Smart women don't play games.* The dictionary defines the word game as *a form of play or sport, a scheme, plan, or trick.* **THE OLD RULES are all about playing games. Why shouldn't you play games in relationships?**

- Playing games is for women who've been convinced that they aren't intelligent enough to figure out the right way to communicate or behave with a man, and instead, must memorize absurd lists of do's and don'ts.

- Playing games is for women who've been warned against using their own natural instincts, and talked into being too mentally frightened to think through situations moment by moment.

- Playing games is for women who've been conditioned to believe the purpose of a relationship is to get the prize—an engagement ring—and that then they'll be the winner.

- Playing games is *stupid*, and you're not stupid.

Games are for children, or people who want to act like children. Good parents teach their children not to lie, not to pretend, not to fool people. Would it be okay with you for your child to play these kinds of games with you? I don't think so. Why, then, would it be okay for you to play these kinds of games with men? It isn't!

Here's what's wrong with playing games in your relationships: *The basis of most games is deception, secrecy, and competition.* If I'm playing a game of cards, I don't want the other person to know what's in my hand—I want the advantage. If I'm playing a game of tennis, I don't want my partner to know where in his court I plan to serve the ball. If I'm playing a game of chess, I want to get more pieces than my opponent.

Deception, secrecy, and competition may be fine for cards, tennis, and chess, but they don't belong in your love life.

You know what men always tell me? They say that one of the reasons women have gotten the reputation of not being as smart as men is that we play stupid games. "Does a woman really think we don't know what's going on when she's playing a game?" men will ask me in disbelief.

Of course a man knows what you're doing. He may even go along with your game for a while, but in the long run, he's not going to respect you for it. And if he really *doesn't* know what's going on, how can you respect *him?* IF A MAN IS STUPID ENOUGH TO FALL FOR OLD RULES GAMES, WHY WOULD YOU WANT HIM?

"Wait a minute," you might be thinking to yourself. "What about those guys who *know what's going on and like it*, men who like women who play games and use the OLD RULES?" As we saw with REAL RULE #3, there are some men who psychologically respond to manipulation. You act indifferent, hard to get, and too busy for him, and suddenly he *has* to have you. Isn't this the result you're hoping for? NO!

Remember: Just because he *wants* you doesn't mean he *loves* you.

I'll bet you've had the experience of wanting something just because you thought you couldn't get it. Example: You break up with a guy, and discover several weeks later that he's dating one of your friends. For a moment, you wonder, "Maybe he wasn't so bad after all . . . maybe I was too hasty." If you're smart, you'll realize that you don't really want him back—you just don't like NOT being able to have him. **Your desire is just a reflexive response from your ego. It's not coming from your heart.**

This is exactly what happens to men when you play games with them, games like:

"You Can't Have Me"

"Maybe I Like You, Maybe I Don't"

"Try to Guess What I'm Doing on the Nights I'm Not Seeing You"

"Aren't I Mysterious."

The men who respond to these games, men who see themselves as the hunter and you as the prey, are men you should stay far away from. Attracting them on purpose is a big mistake.

What's the alternative to playing games and being manipulative? **BEING SMART and BEING APPROPRIATE BY USING THE REAL RULES.**

A Real-Life Scenario of How You Can Use the Real Rules to Check Out a Man

THE SITUATION: You've just started a relationship with a guy you really like, and you don't want to be overly excited about sharing your feelings until you know more about him and how he feels. *One way to approach this is to use the OLD RULES:* never show your enthusiasm when he asks you out, never call him, never return his phone calls, and act nonchalant when he brings you flowers or gifts. In other words, you could play games and TEST HIM.

Here's why this choice isn't just disrespectful, it's risky. By not showing your enthusiasm, never inviting him anywhere, and acting like you couldn't care less about his gifts, you could easily make him think you don't like him and could sabotage the relationship.

Instead, use THE REAL RULES.

Let's say you're having dinner with this man. You could *Ask Questions* (REAL RULE #7) that will help you determine how he feels. You might ask him if he's ever been seriously involved with a woman before, and see how he responds. For example, if he answers: *"No,"* and drops the subject, he's just let you know that he's not used to intimacy, and isn't even comfortable talking about it, both significant warning signs (REAL RULE #10) that you should proceed *very* cautiously.

On the other hand, let's say he answers, *"Yes, I went with a woman for three years in college, but we broke up when we graduated."* He's given you some information and created an opening—**gently ask another question:** *"Did you break up because college was over and you moved away?"* Maybe he'll respond: *"I think so. We were great buddies in school, but we wanted different things from our future, and both realized it wasn't going to work."*

What's your next move? You guessed it—**respond to what he said with whatever is genuine, appropriate, and from your heart.**

For instance, a *compliment:*

"Wow, it's really great that you could both be so honest with one another, and with yourselves about what you wanted. I wish more men were like you."

Or, a *disclosure about yourself:*

"I can really relate to what you're saying. I went through something similar with a guy once. We were together for about a year, and during that time I got really interested in psychology and philosophy through a class I was taking. He thought all that was a waste of time, and even though we really cared for each other, we soon came

to the conclusion that we just weren't compatible, and stopped seeing each other."

Or, an *acknowledgment of what he said and a follow-up question:*

"It must have taken a lot of courage to admit that to each other when you were so close. What were you looking for in your future that was different from what she was looking for?"

What do *your* responses accomplish? A lot!! Here's what they do for him:

- They let him know you appreciate who he is (REAL RULE #16)

- They let him know you are sensitive, intelligent, and compassionate (REAL RULE #5)

- They give him important information about you and your interests (REAL RULE #15)

What do *his* responses do for you?

- They tell you something about his character (REAL RULE #9)

- They give you a clue about what he's looking for in a relationship

- They give you a good idea of his comfort level with intimacy, emotional topics, and honest conversation

Isn't it amazing to see that by using just a few of the REAL RULES in a three minute conversation, you can find out so much about a man?! The information you received in that brief but honest conversation will be much more valuable to you in determining how involved you want to get than if you'd played hard to get and watched how he reacted!

I guarantee you that once you start using THE REAL RULES, and discover how well they work, you'll never doubt it again:

Playing games is the wrong way to get the **right** *man!!*

REAL RULE #5:
Be Yourself

There couldn't be a REAL RULE easier to follow than this one. And yet there's probably no REAL RULE that women ignore more often than this one. BE YOURSELF means just that:

- *Don't try to act like someone you're not.*

- *Don't try to create an image of yourself based on what you think a particular man might like.*

- *Don't try to imitate the kind of woman you've been told men want to marry.*

- *Don't try to behave like your girlfriend just because men are always attracted to her.*

BEING YOURSELF means behaving, communicating, and interacting in ways that are *genuine* for you. For instance, if you're a very enthusiastic, energetic woman, it wouldn't be genuine for you to try not to appear excited when you're having fun with a man. If you're a woman with a great sense of humor, it wouldn't be genuine for you to try not to say anything funny during a four hour date with a guy. If you're a woman who loves intellectual discussions, it wouldn't be genuine for you to try and keep your opinions to yourself during a conversation with your boyfriend.

BEING YOURSELF also means reacting sponta-neously in the moment, rather than from a pre-set list of OLD RULES. If it's being yourself to invite a guy you like to a friend's party even though he's only asked you out once, DO IT. If it's being yourself to share your sadness with a date about a tragedy that befell one of your friends earlier that day even though you won't appear to be "carefree," DO IT. If it's being yourself to spend a half hour on the phone with a guy you're beginning to see as he opens up and shares about his parents' divorce, even though he'll realize you really like him, DO IT.

What's the opposite of being yourself? It's fol-lowing the advice of THE OLD RULES, by **ACTING and HOLDING BACK.**

Acting means:

- Acting cool, even when you care.
- Acting as if everything's great, even when it's not.
- Acting like you're not interested, when you are.
- Acting quiet and reserved, even when you have something to say.
- Acting like you're too busy to see a man, even when you're available.

- Acting "friendly, light and breezy," even if you want to show the deeper part of yourself.

- Acting indifferent when a guy gives you a gift, even if you feel touched and grateful.

Holding Back means:

- Holding back information about your true self, even when a man asks.

- Holding back your feelings, even when he shows his.

- Holding back your opinions.

- Holding back your preferences.

What's wrong with acting and holding back?

1) Whenever you're acting and holding back, you're being dishonest with a man.

The whole premise of THE OLD RULES is that you should only show carefully chosen pieces of yourself to a man so that he doesn't become "turned off" by undesirable parts of your personality, or "scared off" by facts about your life, past and present. You're supposed to act like his ideal woman, and then, once you've got him, you reveal the rest of yourself.

This is a deceptive way to treat a man you're interested in. He thinks you're shy and quiet, only to find out later that it was just an act, you're actually boisterous and expressive. He thinks you're a happy-go-lucky person, only to find out later that you're really introspective and into therapy. He thinks you like the things he likes, only to find out later you have completely different opinions and preferences.

How would you like it if a man acted a certain way for the first few months of your relationship, and once he "got" you, and you had sex with him, he suddenly revealed that he wasn't at all what you thought he was? I think you'd feel furious, conned, and taken advantage of. And you'd be right.

2) Whenever you're acting and holding back, you're being dishonest with yourself.

When you're not being yourself, you're treating yourself with disrespect. It's as if you're saying to your soul, *"I'm ashamed of who you are, so I'm going to hide you until I've got this guy really involved. Then, I'll bring you out of the back room."* **You may temporarily get a man's love by betraying your true self, but you won't get *your own love*.**

3) Whenever you're acting and holding back, you can't relax.

When you practice OLD RULES that inhibit your spontaneity, edit your ability to express yourself, and force you to put on an act, you can't relax. *You can't be really in the moment with your partner, because you're so busy watching yourself.*

Think about something that you really love to do: dancing, singing, participating in a sport, writing poetry, etc. If I told you that for one hour tomorrow, you have to do that activity and stick to a very strict set of rules, and that you'd be judged on the results, I'll bet you wouldn't be too excited. When the time came to do your activity, do you think you'd be having fun? Probably not—instead, you'd be tense, nervous, and fearful, because you'd be worried about doing it "right."

What if I asked you to do the same activity for one hour tomorrow without worrying about doing it "right"? I'll bet you'd relax, be creative and really shine.

This same principle applies to dating. How natural are you going to feel silently counting to five before accepting a date so he doesn't think you're too eager? How relaxed will you be on the phone if you're busy timing the length of the call so that it doesn't last longer then the "prescribed" ten minutes? How anxiety free will you be on a first date trying to remember not to seem too interested, not to look into his eyes but, rather, to stare at your napkin, not to stay longer than a few hours, not to mention that you've been married before, not to answer personal questions directly, not to disagree with anything he says, not to offer your opinion, but to let him take the lead . . . ? I don't know about you, but if I had to remember all that, I'd be a nervous wreck!

4) Whenever you're acting and holding back, you can't trust the love you get.

This may be the most important argument of all for BEING YOURSELF. There's nothing worse than being in an intimate relationship and feeling insecure about your partner's love. *How can you ever trust a man's love if you know you're putting on an act? How can you ever trust that he loves the real you if you're hiding your true self? YOU CAN'T, AND YOU WON'T.*

Remember, THE REAL RULES aren't just about finding a man, they're about finding the *right* man. And in order to find the right man, you have to BE YOURSELF, and see how he reacts.

For instance, if you're a very spiritual or religious person, and you're looking for a partner who has those same values, BE YOURSELF and share this part of your personality in your first few interactions with a man. If he asks you out, and you can't go because that's the night you volunteer at your church, or go to your yoga or meditation class, tell him the truth. Don't just say, "Sorry, I'm busy." He'll have one of three reactions:

1) He'll get turned off and think you're weird, in which case you've just eliminated an incompatible partner.

2) He'll be neutral about it, and continue with the relationship.

3) He'll be really interested in what you're doing, or even reveal that he, too, is very spiritual or religious, which will just deepen your relationship and make it progress even faster.

What's the point of holding back this information until the fourth, fifth, or sixth date, only to find out he's a cynical atheist, or that he thinks meditation is for people who are escaping from the real world? **The sooner you find out if you're compatible, the better.** (See REAL RULE #7 for more ways to do this.)

Loving yourself as a woman means giving yourself permission to BE YOURSELF, and knowing that **if a man doesn't like the real you, then he's NOT for you.**

Actually, BEING YOURSELF is one of the most powerful things you can do to attract the right man. How does it work? The more you *are* yourself, the more relaxed and natural you will be. Guess what happens then? **The more natural and relaxed you are, the more natural and relaxed the right man will feel around you, the more he will want to be with you, until he can't live without you!**

You are unique; you are one of a kind. There is no other woman like you in the whole world. *That's your greatest attribute—your uniqueness. You have no competition when it comes to being you.* Celebrate who you are, let your personality shine, and when the right man finds you, he'll love you for exactly who you are, and feel that God created you especially for him.

REAL RULE #6:
If You Like Someone, Let Him Know

While I was writing this section of THE REAL RULES, I decided to ask a variety of men whether or not they thought a woman should let a guy know she's interested in him. Here are some of their unedited responses:

"If she doesn't let me know she likes me, she might as well forget it, because I'm not setting myself up to chase her."

"I'm so shy that if a woman doesn't somehow show me that she's interested, I'll probably never even get up the courage to talk to her."

"I like relationships that are fifty/fifty. If she's interested, she should let me know, just like I should let her know if I'm interested."

"Let's put it this way—if a woman doesn't let me know she's interested, why would I have anything to do with her?"

"I don't get the question. Why would I want to be with someone who doesn't like me?"

My favorite answer is the last one, because it sums up the whole premise behind REAL RULE #6—**why would a man want to be with you if act like you don't like him?**

Let's say you met a guy through a girlfriend, and you really like him. Because you have mutual acquaintances, you see each other a lot. You want to go out with him, but decide to follow the OLD RULES that say "Don't Talk to a Man First." You also aren't supposed to look at him, smile at him, or appear to be interested in any way. *How in the world is this man supposed to know you like him?* How is he supposed to get up the courage to ask you out when you've shown absolutely no indication that he won't be setting himself up for embarrassment and rejection?

Believe me, no healthy man is going to think the following:

*"Hmmmm, she hasn't said a word to me, she hasn't made eye contact with me, she ignores me when I try to get her attention, and seems completely disinterested in getting to know me . . . **I know, I'll ask her out!!!!"***

When you pretend you're not interested in a man in whom you really ARE interested, you're also setting *yourself* up for disappointment. Unless he has psychic abilities and can read your mind, what makes you think he's going to know you care? Then, when he doesn't approach you, and doesn't call you, you feel totally depressed and conclude, *"I guess he just wasn't attracted to me."* WRONG—You gave him no clues!

Doesn't it make you feel good when a man shows you he's interested in *you*? Don't you feel more confident if he gives you a warm smile, a compliment, or otherwise lets you know he really likes you? Doesn't it make your heart flow? Doesn't it give you permission to take the next step, because you feel safer reciprocating? Of course it does! Then why should you deprive a man you care about of this same experience? (Remember *REAL RULE #1: Treat Men the Way You Want Them to Treat You.*)

Contrary to popular belief, men are HUMAN. They need just as much love and approval as you do. They are just as afraid of rejection as you are. *And perhaps even more than women, men don't like not doing things right or looking bad, so they will* **avoid any situation in which they could feel like they've failed.** The more sensitive a man's heart, the more true this is.

In other words, *the very kind of man you're looking for may* never *approach you first* unless *you give him some kind of opening*—a smile, a friendly comment, an interested look while he's talking . . . SOMETHING.

You'd be surprised at how many men, even those who appear powerful, successful, and confident, are secretly very shy. They're scared to death of being turned down, so they don't even approach women. Some of the most wonderful single men I know are just waiting for the right woman to give them a little encouragement.

Now I'm not saying that regardless of how a man behaves with you, you should stare, fall all over him, grab his arm, make suggestive remarks, and invite yourself over to his apartment. That's not showing your interest—it's being obnoxious and insensitive.

However, you can innocuously and appropriately give a man cues that tell him you would like to get to know him. Then, if after a few tries, he doesn't respond, you should forget about him. Have you lost anything? NO! You've validated another human being by letting him know you enjoy his presence. You've given out a little warmth and love. *Love is never wasted, even if you express it just for a moment.*

What about asking a man you like out on a date? WHY NOT?

a) If he's the right man for you, he'll be flattered, excited, and will probably confess that he'd been wanting to ask you out too.

b) If he's *not* the right man for you, he'll let you know he's not interested, and now you don't have to obsess about him for months—*you know the score and can move on.*

c) And if he's an OLD RULES man, he'll be turned off, and think to himself, *"I liked her until she acted so forward and aggressive. I'm the one who's supposed to be THE MAN . . ."* (Good riddance to this Neanderthal specimen.)

When it comes to beginning a relationship, use common sense. If you ask a man out, have a date, and he doesn't even call you, don't call him again— it's obvious that he's not interested. **There's a big**

difference between showing someone you like him and being pushy and inappropriate.

Remember—acting unattainable *will* **attract some men—THE WRONG MEN.** We've already talked about the kind of unhealthy men who will pursue you if you act like you aren't interested (REAL RULE #3).

- *Men with low self-esteem who feel they deserve to be treated like they're not good enough for you*
- *Men who are unavailable (married, afraid of commitment) and figure you're "safe" if you aren't really interested (See REAL RULE #8)*
- *Old-fashioned men who are turned on by the hunt and want to conquer you*
- *Stupid, insensitive men who can't read your cues to stay away and just don't get it*

You don't want these kind of men in your life, so why put out the bait by acting unattainable and then wonder why you keep attracting the wrong kind of partners?

One final note: It's superstitious nonsense to think that if you make the first move in a relationship by talking to a guy, or even asking him out, it somehow dooms your love affair to failure down the line. If a man really loves you, and wants to spend his life with you, he's not going to say to himself before he proposes, "*Wait a minute . . . didn't she ask me out for coffee first four years ago? Boy, I'm glad I remembered that. I can't marry her. I'm taking this engagement ring back to the store . . .*"

So if you see someone you like, follow your heart: smile at him; compliment him on his shirt; tell him it's nice to see him. And then, wait and see what happens. Who knows—twenty years from now, when people ask your husband how the two of you met, he might say, "*She smiled at me while we were waiting in line to buy coffee, and I fell in love on the spot!*"

REAL RULE #7:
Ask Questions Before You Get Too Involved

Would you lease an apartment without asking the landlord questions about the rent, which utilities are included, and what improvements he's willing to make?

Would you buy a new CD player without asking the salesperson what features it has, and if you'll get a guarantee?

Would you make a reservation at a hotel for your upcoming vacation without asking your travel agent how much it will cost, whether or not the hotel has a pool, and how it's rated?

OF COURSE YOU WOULDN'T, BECAUSE YOU DON'T WANT TO MAKE A MISTAKE. *Then why would you get involved with a man without asking him enough questions so you could be sure you won't end up with the* wrong *person?*

The OLD RULES warn you to not ask questions on the first few dates—God forbid you should appear to be "prying," and you don't want to scare a man off. This is pure nonsense. In fact, the opposite is true.

The first few dates are just when you *should* be asking a guy questions that will help you decide whether or not to get more involved. What's the point of waiting until you're already in love and perhaps sexually intimate to find out the truth about a person? **The time to check someone out is certainly way BEFORE you have sex, and BEFORE you let him into your heart.**

I know what you're thinking—it's not *romantic* to ask questions; it ruins the spontaneity, the excitement, the passion. Well guess what, so does finding out four months later that he's still seeing his ex-girlfriend. So does discovering after you've slept with him that he believes in "open relationships" and has slept with half the cheerleading squad. So does realizing only after you've moved in together that he drinks three beers before noon every day.

Here's another reason we don't ask our new boyfriends more questions: *We don't want to know the answers!!* When you're operating from OLD RULES thinking, your goal is to find a man and marry him. You want to fall in love, not talk yourself out of being with someone. So if you're out on a date with a gorgeous guy and the sexual chemistry is at the boiling point, **you probably aren't going to be interested in finding out anything that might eliminate him!**

When it comes to love, ignorance is NOT bliss. **WHAT YOU DON'T KNOW CAN HURT YOU.** The more information you have about someone, the better you'll be able to judge whether or not this person will make a good mate. The less information you have, the more likely you'll be setting yourself up for anger, disappointment, and heartbreak.

I can't tell you how many women I've worked

with over the years who tell me pathetic, painful
stories about men who hurt them. In the majority of
the cases, these women could have protected themselves from heartbreak and prevented these inci-
dents if they'd just asked more questions before
getting too involved.

What are some of the areas you should ask your
partner questions about in order to make sure he's
right for you?

- Family background and quality of family rela-
  tionships
- Past love relationships and reasons for break-
  ing up
- Lessons learned from life experiences
- Ethics, values, and morals
- Attitudes about love, commitment, communi-
  cation
- Spiritual or religious philosophy
- Personal and professional goals

You'll notice I didn't include issues such as his favorite basketball team, what TV shows he watches, or
his preferences in restaurants. While these topics
may naturally come up in your conversation, they
aren't going to tell you what you really need to
know: *WHAT KIND OF GUY THIS REALLY IS.*

I'm *not* suggesting that you arrive at a first date

with a pad of paper and a pen and say, *"Bill, before we talk about anything else, I have twenty-five questions that I'd like to ask you about yourself."* You shouldn't grill a man about these things; you shouldn't even be appearing to investigate him.

Instead, weave your questions into normal conversation. One way to do this naturally is to let your questions follow from something you share about yourself, or from something you or he is commenting on. The following are some examples of how to do this. Your own conversations will sound a lot better than these, because they'll be real, but the samples will help you get the idea:

- **Family background and quality of family relationships**

  "Since this is our first date, let me tell you a little about myself. I grew up on a farm in Missouri. My Dad sells computer software, and I guess you'd say my Mom was a traditional housewife, although now that the kids are grown, she's going back to school to become a teacher, which I think is great. What about you? **What was your family like?**"

- **Past love relationships and reasons for breaking up**

  "Jill told me you used to go out with her sister. **Was it a serious relationship?**" . . . **OR**

  "It's so nice to be here with you, Steven. I've

been so busy studying for my graduate entrance exams that I haven't really wanted to date anyone for several months. **How have you balanced being in law school and dating?"**

• **Lessons learned from life experiences**

"You mentioned that you were married for a few years when you went into the Navy, to someone you'd known since junior high school. **What's it like to look back on that now?** I know when I look back on my high school relationships, I realize how much I was just trying to get the love I didn't get at home."

• **Ethics, values, and morals**

"You know, I just started a new job at this ad agency, and I'm seeing how when I don't worry about what other people think, I'm so much more creative. I suddenly realize that I'm the only one who ever holds me back. **Have you ever experienced anything like that?"**

• **Attitudes about love, commitment, communication**

"Let me ask your opinion on something, Joe. I was just talking to a girlfriend who's thinking of breaking up with her boyfriend of two years because he says even though he loves her, he isn't ready to marry her. I'm not sure what to tell her—I mean, I'm not a guy so I don't know if he's just making an excuse, or if he's being sincere. **What do you think she should do? What**

do you think might be going on with her boyfriend?''

• **Spiritual or religious philosophy**

''Have you seen that new movie about an an-
gel that moves in with this married couple? It's
actually really cute. I have to admit, I love stuff
like that. I guess you could say I'm a pretty spiritual person. **What do you think—do you believe in a Higher Power, something beyond
what we can see?''**

• **Personal and professional goals**

''Your job with the airlines sounds interesting.
**Do you think you'll stay with that company, or
do you see your career taking another direction?''**

Suppose in the process of asking these questions,
you notice that your date becomes uncomfortable,
evasive, or changes the subject? If you're not sure
that you're reading him right, check by being honest
about what you're observing: (REAL RULE #14):

**''Jim, did I make you uncomfortable when I
asked you about your family?''** or **''Am I right from
your tone of voice that you would rather not talk
about your ex?''** This gives him an opportunity to
clarify what you were picking up, in case he does
want to discuss it, but just felt a little nervous. However, if he confirms that, YES, he wants you to drop
the subject, honor his request. Then when you get

home, give some serious thought to his reactions, and ask yourself if this is the right guy for you.

Once you start putting REAL RULE #7 into practice, you'll be amazed at how much you can find out about someone in a short period of time. Of course, it's only fair that you share about yourself in these areas too, so he can also make sure you're right for him.

Won't it be great to know as much about a man as possible, and *then* decide if you want to become more intimate, see him exclusively and get serious? That's what's so great about THE REAL RULES!!!

REAL RULE #8:
Don't Date Men Who Aren't Completely Available

Every woman has her list of qualities she's looking for in her ideal man: his physical description; his interests; how he treats her; his lifestyle; his love style. But there's one item that we keep forgetting to put on the list, and it's actually the most important qualification of all:

YOUR IDEAL MAN SHOULD BE *AVAILABLE!!!*

Unless you have a self-destructive streak, this shouldn't merely be a desirable quality you'd *like* to find in a man—**it should be an absolute, set-in-stone requirement.**

"Oh, I already know this REAL RULE," you may be thinking to yourself. But let's be honest: how many times have you gotten involved with a man, only to find that he was partially available, or available off and on, depending on whether or not his ex-lover was in town, or that he would be available soon—soon meaning as soon as he decided to tell his wife about you!?

In my book *ASK BARBARA: The 100 Most-Asked Questions About Love, Sex and Relationships,* I define what the word "available" really means, since some of us like to stretch the meaning, rather than eliminating a guy we really like:

Available: Free to be in a relationship with you; not involved with anyone else; not married; not engaged; not going steady; not sleeping with another person; alone; single; all yours.

The following are *not* definitions of available:

With someone, but promises to leave soon

With someone, but he doesn't really love her

With someone, but they're not having sex anymore

With someone, but says he's just staying for the kids

With someone, but she knows about you and it's all right

With someone, and isn't leaving, but wants you to stick around anyway

Just left someone, but might be going back

In other words, STAY AWAY FROM PEOPLE WHO ARE MARRIED, OR IN OTHER RELATIONSHIPS!

There's an easy solution for avoiding these kinds of painful and emotionally traumatic situations: *Practice REAL RULE #8 before you go out on your first date with a man.* That means before you even accept a date, check out his relationship status. HOW? *ASK HIM ABOUT IT DIRECTLY.* If you have any suspicions at all, find out more from mutual friends before dating him, or postpone an official date and have a few more phone calls during which you can ask more questions.

What if a man answers evasively when you question him about his relationship, or after a few dates, you strongly suspect he's been holding something back? STOP DATING HIM IMMEDIATELY, and if he doesn't clear up your concerns, forget about him. You deserve to be with a man who is all yours!

REAL RULE #9:
Look for a Man With Good Character

THIS SITUATION COULD HAPPEN TO YOU . . .

You're single, you're casually dating someone you like, and things are going pretty well. Now you're getting to that phase where you have to decide whether DATING will turn into an exclusive RELATIONSHIP. You know this guy wants a relationship with you, and you've been wanting a relationship with *someone* for a long time, but you're just not sure this man is that someone. You need more time, more dates, more conversations in order to get to know him better.

Thinking about this plan of action, you feel a little anxious. *"How will I know he's right for me?"* you wonder. *"What should I be looking for?"*

REAL RULE #9 is the answer to this dilemma: **LOOK FOR A MAN WITH GOOD CHARACTER.** Why? Because character is one of the most essential qualities you want in a lifelong partner.

What is character? *It's the manifestation of a person's inner self; it's everything he stands for, the values he lives by, the morals that shape his behavior.* A man's character determines how he treats himself, how he treats you, and one day, how he will treat your children. For this reason, good character is the foundation of a good marriage.

What's the difference between a man's *character* and his *personality? Personality is the way someone presents himself to the world.* It's the way he expresses himself on the outside. But a good personality doesn't necessarily indicate that someone has a good character. Don't you know some people who have really fun personalities, but are not very nice people on the inside? Haven't you ever met a man who appeared to be charismatic and charming, only to discover that he was a con artist, with a terrible character? In fact, some people develop elaborately impressive personalities in order to cover up their lack of character.

Character is someone's essence on the inside. It may not express itself as apparently as personality, but it's actually a much truer reflection of who a person really is. If we use the analogy of a relationship being like a cake, then personality is like the icing, and character is the substance.

Here's what most of us do wrong when we apply the OLD RULES

1) We focus on a man's personality traits, instead of checking out his character.

You get to know a guy, and are happy to discover that he loves to travel, has a great sense of humor, is talkative and affectionate. "This could be THE

ONE!'' you tell yourself. But think about it—what do you really know about this man's character? Have you had enough serious discussions to know who he is on the inside? Have you watched for indications of what kind of character he has? Probably not. *You're allowing yourself to be seduced by his personality.*

Won't you be surprised to find out nine months into the relationship that this fun-loving guy is a chronic procrastinator who tries to charm his way through life, and is in severe debt! ''But he was so sweet to me, and so much fun,'' you'll think. You're right; he was fun, but fun won't make him a good husband—character will.

2) We make our goal getting a commitment from a man instead of making sure he's a man with good character.

Remember—the goal of the OLD RULES is to get a man to marry you, hopefully sooner rather than later. If this is your focus, you will only be on the lookout for signs that indicate he wants to commit, or that he doesn't want to commit. Each day becomes about *''Did he call me? Did he tell me he loved me? Did he suggest I meet his parents? Did he make plans for a trip? Did he hint about our future?''*

When you're so busy asking yourself how he feels about you, you forget to ask yourself how YOU feel about HIM: *''How did I feel during that last conversation? Do I like the way he treats other people? Does he respect my opinions and concerns? Do I agree with the way he responds to me when I'm upset with him?"*

I hope you can see the difference between looking for a commitment and looking for the *right man for you*. **Looking for a commitment can make you blind to a man's character.**

Let me tell you the story of a woman who was desperate to get married by the time she was twenty-five. She met a man and practiced all the OLD RULES in her relationship—she played hard to get, acted mysterious, let him run the show. She even had a secret chart with dates by which she wanted certain commitments: One Month to exclusive dating, Four Months to His Saying "I love you," Six Months to His proposing, One Year to marriage. All she focused on was whether or not she was going to make her "deadlines."

Sure enough, five and a half months into the relationship, he proposed, and they got married. Within a year, she was pregnant and soon they had a son. When I met her, she had been married for three years and was completely miserable. She'd come to the conclusion that she didn't even like her husband very much, that he was a totally different person than who she'd thought (or hoped) he was, and she couldn't understand how she'd ended up in such a mess.

"It's not that complicated," I told this poor woman, as her eyes filled with tears. "You went after a commitment—you got a commitment. If you'd gone after a great man with good character, you would have paid attention to a whole different set of events in the relationship. **The proposal was more important to you than the man it was coming from.''**

Here are six important character traits to look for in a man. I teach these in all my seminars, and remind women about them every chance I get:

1. Commitment to Growing and Improving

If you find a man who is committed to growing and improving as a human being, you will have already avoided one of the biggest problems a marriage can face: you want to work on the relationship and he doesn't; you try to talk about the issues and he refuses. Commitment to growth means he wants to learn everything he can about being a better husband and a better person. *You don't have to threaten him to grow. He's doing it on his own.*

2. Emotional Openness

An intimate relationship is not based on sharing a home, a bed, or bathroom. It's based on sharing *feelings*. That's why it's important to look for emotional openness in your partner's character. He'll be a man in touch with his feelings who chooses to express those feelings to you. You should feel that the door to his heart is open, rather than closed.

3. Integrity

Honesty, integrity, and trustworthiness are essential ingredients for a healthy relationship. Knowing that you can count on a man to be truthful with you at all times will give you a tremendous sense of security. Look for signs that he is honest with himself, with you, and with others. You want to respect the way he treats people professionally and personally.

4. Maturity and Responsibility

Good character means a man has grown up and doesn't act like a child, expecting you to take care of him. It also means he is responsible—he does what he says he is going to do in life. He keeps his promises, shows up on time, and respects his word.

5. High Self-Esteem

YOUR PARTNER CAN ONLY LOVE YOU AS MUCH AS HE LOVES HIMSELF. One of the biggest mistakes we make in choosing partners is focusing on how much our mate loves us and how he treats us, and not how he treats himself. Good character means a man feels good about who he is and how he's living his life, rather than walking around apologizing for himself. He takes good care of himself, his body, his environment. He doesn't allow others to mistreat him.

6. Positive Attitude Toward Life

There's an old saying: *"There are two kinds of people*

in the world—positive people and negative people." If you had to spend the rest of your life with one of these kinds of people which would you choose? Make sure your man isn't a negative person always focusing on problems, finding something to complain about, with a cynical attitude. A man with good character sees the goodness in the world, in you and in himself, and you end up feeling good about life when you're with him.

(By the way, don't forget to work on cultivating these same character traits in yourself!)

Remember: I'm not saying that personality and chemistry don't count—they do, but not as much as character. **It's important to like a man for who he is on the outside, but don't stop there. You need to like him even more for who he is on the inside.** Take the time to apply REAL RULE #9 before you get too involved. Then you won't just end up with someone, but with the *right* someone.

REAL RULE #10:
Pay Attention to Warning Signs of Possible Problems

You want to meet a man and fall deeply in love . . .

You want to open up and share the most intimate parts of your heart with him . . .

You want to totally surrender to the passion and magic of the relationship . . .

BUT . . . YOU *DON'T* WANT TO GET HURT. . . .

How can you protect yourself?

The answer is **REAL RULE #10: PAY ATTENTION TO WARNING SIGNS OF POSSIBLE PROBLEMS.**

This is one of the most important REAL RULES, one you need to remind yourself of from your first contact with a man, through your first few dates, and as the relationship becomes more serious. And it's also one of the most difficult to follow. Why? *Because when you meet someone you really like, or find yourself falling in love, you're busy paying attention to other things:*

• How good it feels to finally have someone in your life

- All the fun things you can do as a couple now that you have a boyfriend
- The excitement you feel in your body whenever you think about having sex with him
- Deciding *when* to have sex with him
- Deciding what to wear each time you see him
- Buying new clothes you think he'll like
- Trying to find as much time as possible in your schedule to be with him
- Noticing everything he says to you, everything he does for you, every sign he gives you that he's happy
- Fantasizing about your future together
- Buying him the perfect card, or little gift . . . *you get the picture, because you've done it, and so have I!!!*

The problem is that **when you're preoccupied with these activities, thoughts, and observations, you're probably not paying attention to anything that isn't going well, doesn't look great, or feels uncomfortable.** After all, it's much more fun to go lingerie shopping with your girlfriend in preparation for the first night you'll spend with your boyfriend than to take a walk by yourself and think about the fact that he's been acting a little distant lately.

Why else do we avoid paying attention to warning signs? **BECAUSE WE DON'T WANT TO SEE**

THEM!! *Most of us are looking for reasons to fall in love or to get married,* **not** *reasons to disqualify someone.* This is especially true if:

- You've been single for a long time
- Your biological clock is ticking and you feel time pressure about meeting the right guy
- The guy looks really good on paper (he's a doctor, he has a lot of money, he's really good looking, etc.) (See REAL RULE #11)
- Your friends and family really like him
- You've already had sex with him (See REAL RULE #17)

If these points sound familiar to you, you should force yourself to pay *even more attention*, because you're probably more likely to get caught up in the excitement of a new romance, and talk yourself out of your fears.

Paying attention to warning signs isn't as hard as it sounds. You know that little voice inside your head that whispers to you? It says things like:

"Don't you think he's drinking a little too much tonight?"

"Boy, he sure shut up fast when you asked him about his family!"

"Did you see that? He just made your friend feel terrible by making fun of her."

"Isn't this the third time you've told him you love him, and he hasn't said the words once?"

"Are you imagining it, or is he just a little too forceful in bed?"

"Have you noticed that he's starting to criticize a lot of little things about you, and give you advice about how to run your life?"

"Look—he did it again! That's the third woman he's openly flirted with at this party."

That voice is trying to tell you something—it's saying "PAY ATTENTION!!! Maybe this is a problem, and maybe it's not, but pay attention. I love you and don't want you to get hurt."

The voice you hear, if you stop and listen, is the voice of your own heart and soul. It acts like an inner guide. It's purpose is to always lead you toward your highest good in life. You may experience it not as a voice, but as a "feeling" you have, or an "intuition." But if you're a woman, you know what I'm talking about. And you know what happens when you ignore that voice—*you get yourself in trouble, and you get yourself hurt.*

REMEMBER: MOST OF THE TIME IT'S NOT A MAN WHO DECEIVES YOU, IT'S YOU WHO DECEIVE YOURSELF.

This is the difference between THE OLD RULES and THE REAL RULES. THE OLD RULES give you a long list of artificial do's and don'ts to follow that are supposed to "test" whether or not a man really loves you. You're supposed to time the length of your phone calls, count to five before accepting a date, end dates after a certain amount of hours, not accept dates after a certain day of the week, avoid bringing up certain subjects in conversation, drop his hand when you're walking down the street . . . I mean, come on—*these are dumb ways to tell if a man's right for you.*

THE REAL RULES say: BE YOURSELF (#5) and then PAY ATTENTION (#10) to how he responds. Doesn't that make sense? And it's a lot more relaxing!

If you've been following REAL RULES 1–9, you'll be ready to put REAL RULE #10 into practice. You should know enough about a man by now to stop and evaluate before you go any further.

A special note to women who pride yourselves on always seeing the positive in life, and the good in people: You're going to have to work extra hard to take off your rose-colored glasses and evaluate your man as honestly and objectively as possible. Otherwise, you could be falling in love not with who he really is, but with his potential (See REAL RULE #13).

WHAT SOME WARNING SIGNS COULD MEAN

WARNING SIGN	EVENTUAL PROBLEM
Avoids discussing his past, dodges direct questions.	*Could be hiding something serious;* won't want to work on relationship.
Dislikes talking about feelings. Keeps things light.	*He won't let you in.* Too afraid to get really close.
Won't reveal details of family background. Doesn't see or speak to family much.	*Difficult time being intimate;* might take out hidden anger at them on you.
Giving you much more love and attention than you want to give him.	*He cares more than you do.* Your love is unequal. He'll never be happy.
Giving you much less love and attention than you are giving him.	*You care more than he does.* Your love is unequal. You'll never be happy.
Still in frequent contact with one or more ex's; won't introduce you.	*Not emotionally available.* Won't be able to commit.
Frequent use of alcohol or drugs/can't have sex or fun without them.	*This is an addict* even though he'll deny it. Expect mood swings.
Extremely intense man. You are the center of his life, 24-hours a day.	*He'll be possessive and jealous.* You'll feel controlled and smothered.

WARNING SIGN	**EVENTUAL PROBLEM**
He's a flirt. Attracts women like flies. Needs lots of attention.	*Possible cheater.* You'll never feel secure.
Angry at past lovers. Blames ex's for problems in relationships.	*You're next!* Won't take responsibility for his part in things.
Ongoing credit problems, debts, shaky finances.	*Get out your checkbook!*
Likes to be in charge of everything. He's the boss/ dominant.	*He's a control freak!* You'll start out feeling flattered and end up feeling trapped.
Acts cool, aloof, always together. Never shows vulnerable side.	*He's emotionally unavailable.* You'll never relax and feel safe.
Wants to take care of you completely. Acts fatherly and protective.	*He'll always pull rank.* You'll never feel competent enough. He'll treat you like a child.
Really into sex. Has to have it all the time.	*He's sexually addicted.* Can't be intimate without it. You'll feel used (and sore).

This list is just an example of the kinds of warning signs you may notice, and what they might mean. There are obviously hundreds more, and if you're paying attention, you'll notice them. What should you do if you see a warning sign? DON'T do the following:

Minimize its importance—"He really doesn't drink that much, mostly on weekends, and besides, it's just beer."

Make excuses for him—"I know he seems overly jealous and possessive, but his ex-wife cheated on him and made him really insecure."

Rationalize—"He's not really flirting. See, since he's in sales, he's trained to be a really friendly person, especially to women."

Deny it—"What do you mean, you think he doesn't treat me well? He's wonderful to me. No one's ever loved me the way he does. You're just jealous that I'm happy and you're not."

Retreat into Fantasyland—"I realize he has a real problem with intimacy, but I'm sure that once we're engaged, it will disappear."

What *should* you do if you notice a warning sign?

Communicate honestly about how you feel and what you're concerned about (REAL RULE #14). Either the problem will resolve itself, and the warning sign will disappear, or it won't, and it's time to move on.

REAL RULE #11:
Judge a Man by the Size of His Heart, Not by the Size of His Wallet

"Barbara, I'm so tired of dating men who turn out to be jerks. Aren't there any nice guys out there? How do I find them?"

I must hear this from women dozens of times a week. And I'll tell you what I tell them:

Stop limiting yourself to dates with guys who look "good on paper" . . .

Stop eliminating men just because they don't "fit your picture" of the perfect catch . . .

Stop judging men by the size of their wallets, and instead . . .

Start looking for a man with a big heart.

Believe me, I realize this is easier said than done. I know your mother told you, "It's as easy to fall in love with a rich man as a poor man." I know that we live in a very materialistic society where there's so much emphasis placed on outer wealth and accomplishment, *rather than inner wealth and accomplishment*. I know the fantasies and fairy tales you grew up with told you that it was the handsome prince, *not* the stable boy, who swept the princess off her feet and installed her in the palace to live happily ever after.

But let's get real. This isn't the eighteenth or nine-teenth century, where women had no money, no property of their own, and a woman was forced to marry based on the material security a man could give her, and not on how much he loved her and she loved him. This is almost the twenty-first century. Times have changed, thank God. Unlike your great-great-grandmother and millions of women who went before you, you are free to marry whomever you want!!

Some things, however, have not changed. Men, in particular, are still evaluated by their:

- Money
- Lifestyle
- Power
- Career
- Reputation

And too many women still consciously or uncon-sciously are the harshest judges.

When a woman tells a female friend that she's in-volved with a new man, the friend's first response will most likely be:
"What does he do for a living?"
And when a woman meets another woman, and finds out that she has a boyfriend, or is married, she will probably ask:
"What does your husband do?"

I've often heard women respond to this question apologetically if they don't feel their partner's profession is prestigious enough. "Oh, he's just a salesman," or "Well, right now he works in a clothing store, but he's taking classes to get into real estate." And how many of us have heard our parents or grandparents discussing a woman who *"married well,"* not meaning that she had found a caring, loving man, but that she'd married a man with a good career, a prestigious job, or lots of money.

Recently, I was at a party and overheard a woman talking to a few of her friends about a guy she was dating. *"He's the best!"* she shared excitedly. *"He has a gorgeous town house in the city, and a country home upstate. He's already taken me on three trips, one to Aspen, one to a health spa, and one to Mexico. And look at this bracelet he gave me—diamonds and rubies, and it's only been three months. I'm just so in love. Of course, I'm playing it very cool, and not letting him know how I really feel. I'm saving that for when he pulls out an engagement ring."*

I felt ill listening to this woman's conversation. In my opinion, she wasn't much different from a high class whore. I know those are strong words, but think about it: she expects payment for her love, and he gives it to her. The more he pays, the more she gives. Sounds like a hooker to me . . .

It makes me sad that, as women, we have been so disempowered throughout history that many of us still look for sex with a rich man, or a husband with an important job and standing in the community, or a boyfriend with a nice car and a condo to make us feel worthwhile **rather than finding our own worth within ourselves.** Sure, there are millions of us who are helping to support our families, or even doing it alone. *But there are just as many women who place exaggerated value on the money and prestige a man can offer us and, in the process, neglect to discover what kind of heart and soul our prospective partner possesses.*

Money cannot make you happy. It can make you comfortable, but it can never fill up your heart. I know so many women who allowed themselves to be seduced by a man's money and power, only to find themselves trapped in empty, miserable marriages. These are women who would give all of their fine jewelry, expensive furniture, and elaborate vacations just to have the experience of real love, passionate sex, and shared intimacy. I'm not saying that money will make you *unhappy*, just that if you don't have the love and compatibility to go along with it, money won't be enough.

I have an old friend who just can't seem to find the right man. She can't figure out why, but to me it's obvious—**she won't even go out with a man who isn't well off and living a flashy lifestyle.** She looks for guys with fancy cars, high profile jobs, and expensive habits. Whenever I ask her how things are going with her latest date, *she tells me where they ate or what they did, and not how she feels.* This material thrill lasts for a few months, and then inevitably, she has to face the fact that this guy can't express his feelings, or is very self-centered, or is scared to death of making a commitment. She breaks up with him, waits a few weeks, and starts the cycle all over again when the next man with a Porsche comes along.

REAL RULE #11 says that: WHEN YOU CHOOSE A MAN BASED ON WHAT HE CAN OFFER YOU MATERIALLY, RATHER THAN WHAT HE CAN OFFER YOU EMOTIONALLY, YOU WILL END UP IN THE WRONG RELATIONSHIP.

Beside, don't you hate it when certain men judge you on the size of your breasts? Then don't judge them on the size of their paycheck.

Of course, there are wonderful men out there who are financially successful *and* are also warm, loving human beings. If your true love happens to also be rich or powerful, that's great. *But here's the good news:*

There are even more men who don't have a lot of money, don't drive fancy cars, and don't do something exciting for a living who are **honest, trustworthy, loyal, romantic, longing to get married and have kids, and are ready to love and adore you** **right now,** *if only you'll notice them, and give them a chance.*

You see, there is one thing you should expect a man to give you, but it's not money, power, or prestige—**it's LOVE.** That's why THE REAL RULES are all about paying attention to the size of a man's heart.

REAL RULE #12:
Be Fair: Don't Practice Double Standards

If there's one rule in life that we, as women should really understand, it's REAL RULE #12. After all, women know what it's like when the rules aren't fair:

- Women make up 50 percent of the world's population, are responsible for two thirds of all hours worked, *but make only one tenth of the income that men do.*

- Women own less than 1 percent of the world's property.

- Women earn about 69 cents to every $1.00 men make for performing the same jobs.

- There's only one job in America where women earn more than men: PROSTITUTION.

These statistics are true, but they aren't fair. Most women don't need studies to tell us this. We know it from our own experience, working twice as hard as men to get ahead in business, being called pushy and aggressive when we're powerful instead of being admired as a leader, trying to break through the glass ceiling and not just excel at "women's jobs," but have opportunities to excel at any job.

There's another phrase to describe a situation where there's one set of rules for one group and one set for another: **A DOUBLE STANDARD.** Double standards aren't fair because they don't apply the rules of life equally to all people.

The old ways in love and life and the OLD RULES that come from them are based on double standards and lack of fairness. For instance, here are some of the OLD RULES, and I'm not making these up.

- *Make a man pay for everything—don't even offer to split a check, even if you have much more money than he does.*

- *Never meet a man halfway, even if it's totally inconvenient for him to come pick you up.*

- *Don't call a man, even if he calls you and asks you to call back.*

- *Don't worry about making a man upset and angry— it just means that he's crazy about you.*

- *Stop dating a man if he doesn't buy you a romantic gift—ideally jewelry—for your birthday or Valentine's Day.*

- *Stay emotionally cool in bed so he doesn't think you're too crazy about him.*

- *When a man is at your place, pretend phone calls from your girlfriend are calls from a guy so he gets jealous.*

- *Don't initiate sex—it will emasculate him.*
- *Men propose when they're afraid of losing you, so threaten to move out of town, or become distant and difficult if you want him to ask you to marry him.*

Do these suggestions sound FAIR to you? Do they even sound sane? *They're not just double standards—they're disrespectful, immoral standards.* Imagine how you'd feel if a man tried these disgusting, manipulative behaviors on you: hopefully, you'd be out of there in a flash. So why would you want to behave this way in a relationship?

You have a chance, in your own life, to take a stand for the cause of equality in the world. How? *By being fair in your relationships with men and not applying any double standards of your own.* It just takes a little sensitivity and common sense. FOR INSTANCE:

- **Deal with the money issues in your relationship in a FAIR and equitable manner.** Why should the man pay for everything, especially if you're both working? Even if he has much more money than you do, it's a loving gesture to take care of him once in a while. Of course, as with all the REAL RULES, the best solution is to discuss this issue with a man and come to a solution that feels good to both of you. (You'll also learn a lot about him by discussing money issues—an added bonus)

- **Respect a man's time and obligations.** There's nothing wrong with having a guy come pick you up for a first date, if that's what you both want. But it's inconsiderate, selfish, and yes, RUDE, to always expect him to go out of his way for you. Why should he? Are you better than him? Why would he even consider marrying such an inconsiderate, self-centered woman? If you have plans to go to a movie, and he happens to have an appointment late in the day near the movie theater, it only makes sense for you to meet him there. *The right man will respect you for respecting him.*

- **If you want to call a man, go ahead. And if he calls you, for goodness sake, call him back.** There is absolutely nothing wrong with calling a man you're dating, unless you're calling him every night and he only calls you once a week, or not at all. If you practice the other REAL RULES, PAY ATTENTION (#10) and DON'T PLAY GAMES (#4), then your phone calls will be appropriate. And unless you want to appear stuck up and rude return his calls promptly. What would *you* think of a guy who ignored your calls . . . ?

I think you get the idea. Treat him as you want him to treat you (REAL RULE #1). And if you're ever tempted to give in to an OLD RULE (such as leaving him if he doesn't give you jewelry for your birthday), STOP AND THINK ABOUT THE FLIP

SIDE OF THE DOUBLE STANDARD (he should leave you if you don't give him sex). That will snap you back to reality real quick, and you can try a REAL RULE instead!

REAL RULE #13:
Don't Fall in Love With a Man's Potential

One of the greatest talents women possess *is the ability to see the potential in things, to make something from nothing.* You walk into an empty studio apartment with a friend who's thinking about renting it, and you can visualize exactly what she could do to make the place warm and inviting. You find out that three friends are coming over for dinner in half an hour, and you somehow throw together what's in your cupboards and refrigerator to make a great meal. You're invited to a wedding at the last minute, and with the help of some accessories and jewelry, you turn your plain black dress into a fancy looking outfit.

This quality is wonderful when it comes to entertaining or redecorating, but it's dangerous when you try to apply it to your love life. I call it **FALLING IN LOVE WITH A MAN'S POTENTIAL.**

You know how it works—you meet a guy who seems really nice, and you like him a lot. Pretty soon, however, you realize that *he's "a fixer-upper"; he's going to need a lot of work to become the kind of man you'd want to marry.* Maybe he's too quiet and shy for you, but you're sure that, deep inside, there's a powerful, expressive person dying to emerge. Maybe he's still recovering from a bad breakup, and isn't ready to give you his heart, but you just know that, in time, he could learn to trust you, and love again. Maybe he's a frustrated musician who can't seem to get his career going, and you're positive that he could be rich and famous, if only someone would give him a chance.

Here's the problem: **You aren't in love with who he actually is—you are in love with who you hope he will become.** And of course, who's going to help him become the great guy you know he can be? Why, you, of course! You'll be his cheerleader, his hero, his savior, his inspiration. You secretly think to yourself, *"He just needs someone to believe in him, and that someone is me. My love will heal him, and, yes, make him the man he's destined to become."* RIGHT? **WRONG!!!**

Another form of falling in love with a guy's potential is going on an "emotional rescue mission." You find someone who seems wounded, fragile, unloved, and you feel irresistibly drawn to caring for that person. He feels so grateful, and you feel so noble. Before you know it, you're in a relationship that looks more like a therapy session than a healthy, balanced love affair. And once you're in it, it's *really* hard to get out without feeling incredibly guilty, or like you're abandoning him.

What's wrong with these scenarios? Several things:

1) When you're in love with a man's potential, you're not looking at him as a *person*—you see him as a *project*. He's a goal on your "to do" list . . . TUESDAY: FIX JIM.

2) He didn't ask you to help him, fix him, or rescue him.

In fact, maybe he doesn't even want to change. When you fall in love with a man's potential, you're setting yourself up to be his mother, his teacher, his therapist, but not his lover.

3) You can end up wasting a lot of time with the wrong person.

When you're in love with a guy's potential, your relationship is based on your belief that he will change, or open up or get a job or stop drinking or heal his pain, whatever it is you want him to do. *Unless your boyfriend has specifically told you that he is taking positive steps toward making the change you're hoping for, and you see results from those steps*, you're wasting your time. Staying in the wrong relationship is unfair to you and also unfair to him.

REAL RULE #13 says: Men aren't items like paintings or antiques—so don't choose a man for his "investment quality." If you begin a relationship with someone, make sure you *love, respect, and enjoy him as he is today, rather than loving who you hope he'll become in the future.* It's okay to have preferences of how you'd like to see him grow, but he should be *enough* for you as he is *right now.*

Part 3

THE REAL RULES FOR FOR COMMUNICATING WITH MEN

REAL RULE #14:
Be Honest About Your Feelings

After reading about all the REAL RULES for finding the right relationship, such as Don't Play Games (#4), Be Yourself (#5), If You Like Someone, Let Him Know (#6), and Be Fair (#12), this first REAL RULE for communication should come as no surprise to you: **BE HONEST ABOUT YOUR FEELINGS.**

Believe me, I've spent years and years studying communication between men and women, teaching classes and seminars on the subject, and working personally with thousands of couples, and I always come back to the same conclusion: **communication that works always has honesty as its foundation. It's when you're dishonest about how you feel in relationships that things get messy, unpleasant, and complicated.**

This is one of the biggest problems I have with THE OLD RULES—they're based on emotional dishonesty . . . acting, pretending, withholding, even lying.

THE REAL RULES say that you should always be honest about your feelings. I call that *Emotional Honesty.* Naturally, you have to integrate your honesty with common sense. For instance, I don't suggest walking up to a guy at a party whom you've never spoken to before and saying: "Excuse me, I just want to be emotionally honest and let you know that your ass looks great in those jeans, and I feel like dragging you into the bedroom and screwing your brains out." That goes way, way, way beyond honesty! The emotional honesty I'm talking about is the kind you either do or don't express to a man at different stages of an intimate relationship.

What's Right About Emotional Honesty and What's Wrong With Emotional Dishonesty

1. Emotional Honesty Creates Intimacy

Have you ever had a talk with someone in which you were both really honest about yourselves with one another? How did you feel afterwards? CLOSER. That's because emotional honesty creates instant intimacy. Honesty builds a bridge between your heart and the heart of the person you're sharing with. It's as if honesty opens the door to your heart so a man can feel the real you inside.

What should you be emotionally honest about? *Whatever is true for you.* For instance, if a guy calls and you're happy to hear from him, say just that: *"I'm really happy to hear from you."* If he asks you out and you're excited, say *"I'm really looking forward to getting to know you better."* If you're having a great conversation during dinner, say *"I can't tell you how much I'm enjoying this conversation—I love the way your mind works!"* It's a lot simpler to remember to be emotionally honest than to follow the OLD RULES and try *not* to say anything that may make you seem attainable.

If you aren't emotionally honest with a man you're involved with, you'll find the relationship staying on a superficial level, and never really deepening into something more serious. The more you both share, the more intimacy you'll experience, and the more likely you'll be to create a future together.

2. Your Emotional Honesty Gives Your Partner Permission to Open Up

When you are emotionally honest with a man, it gives him permission to be emotionally honest with you. It makes it safer for him to talk from his heart, something many men feel awkward doing. If a man senses that you're holding back, he'll keep his guard up. He can't open up if he can't feel you, even if he wants to get closer.

When you practice REAL RULE #14 and share your feelings, his trust in you builds, and his walls come down. Why wait for him to be the first person to open the door? You could wait forever. Remember, most (not all) men are less comfortable sharing feelings than most women. So reach out with honesty. No matter what happens, you can't lose—**an** honest man who's right for you will always respect you for being emotionally honest.

3. Emotional Honesty Prevents Misunderstandings That Could Sabotage Your Relationship

Imagine a man and a woman who've been dating for a month. Both of them really like each other, *but both are playing hard to get, acting aloof, pretending they're too busy to see one another much—in other words, they're being emotionally dishonest.* She's thinking: "He obviously doesn't like me very much. I probably should stop seeing him." He's thinking: "She seems so cold when she's with me. I'll bet I'm not her type at all. I probably shouldn't call her again." The relationship ends, and **neither of them will ever know that their emotional dishonesty sabotaged what could have been true love.**

Pretending you don't feel something that you do feel rips you off, and it rips the other person off. *Do you really want to risk turning off a guy who may be the right one for you by acting cool and unattainable?*

4. Emotional Dishonesty Reinforces Negative Character Traits

Holding back your good feelings about someone trains you to be emotionally dishonest with everyone. Soon you forget how you really feel—you're so busy putting on an act. Society is already filled with too many people like that.

5. Emotional Dishonesty Can Attract the Wrong Man Into Your Life

Remember REAL RULE #3: There are men you *don't* want to end up with who will love it if you're emotionally dishonest, and if your feelings remain hidden. These are the same guys that the OLD RULES foolishly warn you will get "bored" with you if you reveal too much. I say, go ahead and reveal away! The kind of man who needs to be kept constantly stimulated like a restless two year old is NOT going to make a good husband, a good boyfriend, or even a good date. Why waste your time with one of these immature bozos? *Being emotionally honest is one of the best ways to screen out emotionally frightened men. Just open up, and watch them run!*

On the next page is a chart to keep you inspired and help you remember why REAL RULE #14 is one of the most important rules of all.

GOOD MEN HATE . . .	**GOOD MEN LOVE . . .**
When you secretly test him to see if he's who you want	When you're honest about what you expect and what you're looking for
When you pretend you don't care, to see if he'll chase after you	When you let him know where he stands so he can feel safe in the relationship
When you act unimpressed with him and his efforts to woo you	When you share your enthusiasm for him and his efforts
When you act like he's not making an impact on you	When you express how good he makes you feel
When your distance makes him feel it's not safe for him to get more involved	When you open your heart and share the truth so he can feel safe enough to get even more serious about you

One last piece of advice: Don't forget to use REAL RULE #10 (PAY ATTENTION) as you practice emotional honesty. If you pay attention to how your partner responds each time you interact, you'll find a good balance between being open and being appropriate.

REAL RULE #15:
Show Your Most Attractive Feature—Your Mind

What's your sexiest, most attractive feature? You might think it's your hair, your breasts, your legs, or your skin, but you're wrong—**IT'S YOUR MIND.**

When a man falls in love with your mind, he's falling in love with your essence, your uniqueness, the secret behind the woman on the outside. Think about it . . . What would you be without your mind? A body made of skin, hair, bones, an empty shell just lying there devoid of passion, devoid of life. If your mind were gone, you wouldn't be *"you,"* because your mind is the source of your *"youness."*

Your mind is like the express train that takes a man deep into your being, until he can feel your heart. This is why REAL RULE #15 advises that you want a man to fall in love with your mind, and not just your body. After all, as you age, your body will inevitably change, and become less and less the "ideal." But the opposite happens to your mind—*as you get older, it will grow in richness, in understanding, and in wisdom.*

How can you get a man to fall in love with your mind? You have to show it to him by practicing REAL RULE #15. **You have to use words to express**

who you really are so he can know your mind and think it's wonderful. You have to share your opinions, your thoughts, your dreams, and your insights. The things you say have to be genuine reflections of who you are and how you feel. When you do this, the right man for you will be enchanted by your mind. You'll become his best friend, his closest confidante, and the woman he wants to spend his life with.

What should you talk about? That question itself is *unnecessary. You should talk about whatever you want, whatever is true and important to you from moment to moment.* Remember, BE YOURSELF (REAL RULE #5). If you have to edit what you want to say every five minutes, you'll be tense, insecure, and fearful, and the relationship will be exhausting. In fact, isn't that why you often feel nervous talking to a man you like? Instead of talking with him the same way you'd talk to anyone, you suddenly feel under pressure, like there's a wrong and right way to be. Naturally, you can't be yourself.

For example, let's say you're a first grade teacher and you love kids. You're out on a date and recall something really cute that one of the kids did in class that day. Share it with the man you're with—it's what you care about; it's who you are. Of course, according to the OLD RULES, you shouldn't bring up anything that could give him "the wrong idea" about you (whatever that is). **I say, bring up whatever feels right, and if it turns this guy off, so be it.**

What's the alternative to this? You know by now that the OLD RULES suggest the opposite of REAL RULE #15: On a date you're supposed to be quiet and reserved, light, charming, and mysterious, "like a summer breeze." (More like an empty brain with the wind blowing through it, in my opinion.) You sit there, a mysterious, zombielike doll, nodding your head at everything he says, appearing interested in his life, but not revealing yours. Then, after keeping this up for several months so that he finds your mystery irresistible, you finally bring up how you feel about your job and how much you love working with children, only to have him respond: *"Most kids are just annoying brats. They give me the creeps."*

Well, after weeks and weeks of trying to be what he wanted, you just found out that you can't even talk about your job with this man, and worse, that he hates kids. **You've just wasted months of your life by not practicing REAL RULE #15. If you'd shown this moron your mind on the first date, you would have discovered something about *his* mind that showed you he was the wrong guy for you, and you could have ended things immediately.** Remember the premise of THE REAL RULES: *Your goal is to find the* right *man, not just a man.*

WHAT'S THE POINT OF EVER HIDING YOUR TRUE FEELINGS, YOUR INTERESTS, YOUR OPINIONS FROM A MAN? How is a guy going to know who he's sitting there with if you are editing yourself and trying to look like someone you're not? *And how are you going to know he's fallen in love with the REAL YOU?* You won't.

What about disagreements? How does REAL RULE #15 suggest you handle situations in which revealing what's on your mind could create conflict with a man you like? You know what I'm going to say: **SO WHAT IF HE'S UNCOMFORTABLE WITH SOMETHING YOU SAY OR FEEL? YOUR JOB IN LIFE IS *NOT* TO MAKE HIM COMFORTABLE— IT'S TO *BE TRUE TO YOURSELF***

Let's look at an example: you and your date are discussing mutual friends who just broke up. Your date says, *"From what Bob told me, Julie is taking the breakup really hard."* Now, you know for a fact (since Julie called you last night) that Bob didn't even have the guts to end the nine-month relationship in person—he did it by leaving a message on her answering machine! So you respond:

"Of course, she's upset. After all, Bob was a jerk—he broke up with her by leaving her a message! I think that's pretty cowardly. Julie not only feels rejected, she feels like nothing they had together really meant anything to Bob."

Instantly, you can tell from the fact that your boyfriend is scowling at you that he doesn't like what you just said. *"You women always stick together, don't you?"* he retorts sarcastically.

Okay . . . let's stop this scene for a moment, and I'll ask you: **How should you respond at this point in the conversation?** Remember, you really like this guy, and want to continue seeing him. On the other hand, he's just said something you totally disagree with. What do you do?

OLD RULES: *Smile, back off the delicate subject, and don't say anything more about how you feel, because above all, you want to appear "easy to be with."*

REAL RULES: *Respond to what he said honestly, without hostility or judgment, letting him know how you really feel: "I can tell from your tone of voice that what I said upset you. I didn't mean to attack Bob— I always liked him. But I do feel that he could have been more respectful to Julie, and told her in person, even though that's a scary thing to do."*

At this point, your date will either engage in a dialogue with you about how we should treat each other in relationships, and you'll learn more about each other and emerge from the conversation feeling even closer, OR, he will get more and more uncomfortable, giving you the message that he is rigid in his opinions and doesn't want to talk about it. **You'll either be one step closer to seeing that he's the right man, or one step closer to seeing that he's the wrong man.**

REAL RULE #15 says: Never compromise your values or edit your opinions in order to get a man to like you. When you sacrifice your own integrity, you lose a piece of yourself, and one day, you wake up and don't know who you are anymore. If he really loves you, he'll love the way your mind works, even when he disagrees with the specific content!!

This same principle applies to the OLD RULE advice that you should hide your interests or beliefs in the beginning of a relationship so that you don't "scare a man off." **The OLD RULES say:** If you read self-help books, hide them when he comes over. If you are in recovery from alcoholism, don't mention that you've ever attended AA meetings. If you've been to a therapist, don't bring it up. If you have an interest you feel he might not like (astrology, Bible studies, kick-boxing, or whatever), avoid talking about it until much later in the relationship.

WRONG, WRONG, WRONG. You should talk about whatever you want to talk about. You should show him your mind and its interests, and, as I've said over and over (but we can never hear it enough!), *if he doesn't like who you are, and how your mind thinks, he is wrong for you.*

My husband loves my mind, even when he doesn't always agree with me. When I'm working hard on a book, and don't even bother to get dressed or wash my hair, he still loves me, because he loves my mind. When I'm sick, and cannot be his lover or his date, he still loves me, because he loves my mind. And I know that when I'm very old and physically frail with wrinkles and long white hair, he'll still love me, because he loves my mind.

You, too, deserve to have a man who loves your mind. Remember—it's taken women thousands of years to earn the right to express our opinions, state our preferences, and use our voice. Take advantage of this right that so many women before you fought to get, and proudly share your mind with men. One day, the right man will whisper to you: *"I've been waiting all my life to meet a woman with a mind like yours."*

REAL RULE #16:
Be Emotionally Generous, Not Emotionally Stingy

If I took a survey of all the men that you've ever been involved with, and asked them the following question about you, what do you think the results would be?

Is *(your name)* more of an "EMOTIONALLY GENEROUS" woman, or an "EMOTIONALLY STINGY" woman?

Before you rush into an answer, think about it . . . *to be **emotionally generous** means to give abundantly and freely of your love, your praise, your affection, and your appreciation. To be **emotionally stingy** is the opposite—to give sparingly and very conditionally of your love, your praise, your affection, and your appreciation when in a relationship.*

Emotionally stingy women are usually following some form of the OLD RULES, which advise you to *treat a man not like a person to be respected, but a prize to be won.* In fact, the OLD RULES warn you against appearing too interested, eager, or enthusiastic in your relationship (even with your own husband!), and counsel you to, instead, act nonchalant, cool, and aloof.

But here's the problem: **When you consciously**

withhold the "reward" of verbal appreciation, physical affection, and other forms of loving behavior until the man "performs" properly by chasing you, giving you the right gifts, and proving that he "deserves" your praise *you're treating him like a trained pet, not a human being.* You may not intend to be emotionally stingy, but that's exactly how you appear when you dole out your compliments and expressions of caring like they're doggy treats!

If you've been an emotionally stingy woman with your men, then REAL RULE #16 is important for you to understand and practice. And if you're an emotionally generous woman, you probably already know REAL RULE #16 in your heart.

Remember the essence of REAL RULE #2—*that men need as much love and reassurance as you do?* **Well, REAL RULE #16 says: don't just think, "Oh, I know men are like that." DO SOMETHING ABOUT IT by sharing your appreciation and gratitude with the man you care for. Be *emotionally generous* with him.**

I'm obviously not suggesting that on a first date, you shower a man with romantic cards, complement him every five minutes, and thank him twenty-five times for dinner. This isn't being emotionally generous—it's emotionally drowning someone! As with all the REAL RULES, REAL RULE #16 is based on a balance between being yourself *and* being appropriate in the moment.

Here are some ways to put REAL RULE #16 into practice:

1. Appreciate a Man With Your Words

Women always complain that men don't use enough words to let us know how they feel, and yet many of us are just as guilty because we assume men don't need to hear these things, and so we become verbally stingy. *Men not only love to know you appreciate them—they need to know it in order to open their hearts to you.*

- **Use words to tell him what he does right.** If he calls to say he'll be five minutes late, appreciate him for his consideration. If he gives you a pep talk about your upcoming job interview, appreciate him for supporting you and understanding how you feel.

- **Use words to tell him what you like about his character.** If he listens to your feedback without getting defensive, appreciate his willingness to improve himself. If he slows down while driving to let another car in front of him, appreciate how courteous he is.

- **Use words to appreciate any feelings about you he expresses, or steps of commitment he takes.** If he tells you that you look beautiful, let him know how good that makes you feel. If he tells you he wants to introduce you to his best friend so you can get to know each other, use words to let him know how happy you are that he wants to share parts of his life with you.

The more words of appreciation you use, the more cues you will be giving a man about what he's doing right so he can keep doing it! After all, how else is he supposed to get to know your likes and dislikes . . . unless you use words to tell him?! How else is he supposed to know how he's doing in the relationship . . . unless you use words to tell him? *Don't forget—the right man wants to make you happy, and will appreciate you for letting him know he's accomplishing his goal.*

2. Show Your Gratitude

If there's one thing men hate, it's women who are spoiled, unappreciative, and ungrateful, women who act like a man's calls, gifts, thoughtfulness, and presence in their lives are no big deal. Why would an emotionally healthy man want to spend his life with you if you act like nothing he does is ever quite good enough? He wouldn't.

- **Thank him for his acts of kindness and consideration.** If he goes out of his way to plan an evening filled with specific activities he knows you enjoy, thank him for being so thoughtful. If he calls you to wish you good luck on an exam,

or in making a presentation at work, thank him
for thinking of you.

- **Thank him for what he gives you materially
  and emotionally.** If *he* takes *you* to a concert or a
  movie, thank him for making the plans and inviting you to be his guest. If he brings you flowers, thank him genuinely for them, and put them
  in your nicest vase in a prominent spot. If he
  shares his feelings with you, thank him for being
  so open.

- **Express your gratitude by reciprocating with
  kindness and consideration of your own.** If he's
  gone out of his way several times to take you to
  your favorite activities on dates, plan a surprise
  for him featuring something you know he enjoys. If he has been very supportive of your career goals and called you at work to give you
  encouragement, call him to wish him good luck
  on an important day.

Expressing appreciation and showing gratitude
are practices I believe we should apply in all of our
relationships. However, when you're starting an intimate relationship with a man, appreciation and gratitude are especially crucial. Remember: *men hate
feeling like they're not doing it right, whatever "it" is.*
This is the secret to REAL RULE #16, and why following it is the key to a happy courtship and even-
tual engagement: **The better a job your man feels**

he's doing in your relationship, the more confident and eager he'll be to make a *permanent commitment!!*

If you're like most women, you love when a man appreciates everything about you, from the smallest detail of your outfit to the way you make him feel. And you love when he doesn't take you for granted, and instead, shares his gratitude for all you do for him. On the contrary, there's nothing worse than a selfish, spoiled, narcissistic man who thinks your job is to be his cook, his maid, his cheering squad, and his on-call-24-hours-a-day sex toy, yet who never says thank you and makes you feel you're never doing it quite right.

I remind you of this so that, once again, you can remind *yourself* to treat a man as you'd have him treat you. **The right man for you will love and respect you for being emotionally generous, and he'll be emotionally generous back.** The right man for you will think to himself, *"That's the kind of warm, giving woman I'd want to be married to. That's the kind of caring, sensitive person who would make a great Mom someday."* So make sure the right man knows you're right for him by practicing REAL RULE #16 and sharing your emotionally generous heart.

Part 4

THE REAL RULES
ABOUT SEX

REAL RULE #17:
Wait Until You Are Emotionally Intimate Before Becoming Sexually Intimate

Have you ever told yourself that you were madly in love with a guy, and after having sex with him, realized that what you were feeling wasn't love, but lust?

Have you ever slept with the wrong man too soon, but went on to have a relationship with him anyway just to "legitimize" the sex, so you wouldn't look like a tramp?

Have you ever had sex with a man who you're angry at yourself for ever getting involved with, or who you are too embarrassed (or grossed out) to even want to remember?

If you answered "yes" to any of these questions, or have had similar experiences, it was probably because you didn't know about (or ignored) **REAL RULE #17: Wait until you're emotionally intimate with a man before becoming sexually intimate.** Having sex too soon is one of the most common and most hurtful mistakes women make in their relationships with men.

What do I mean by "too soon"? It's not about a certain time period, like ten dates, or three months. *REAL RULE #17 emphasizes that you should base this important decision about becoming sexually intimate with a man* not *on how much time has passed, but instead,* **on how much true emotional closeness and compatibility has been established between you.**

Making love is one of the most powerful experiences two people can share with one another. At its best, it is the union not only of physical bodies, but of hearts and spirits as well. When you make love with a man, you're not just merging with his form—you're opening yourself up to receive his energy, his vibration, the essence of who he is into your own body. Depending on who you end up in bed with, this energy can either have a wonderful effect on you, or an awful effect on you.

Doesn't this explain why you may have had the experience of thinking you really liked someone, finally making love with him and enjoying it, but almost immediately following the sex, finding yourself totally turned off to him? It's as if, once the lust dissolved, you were left feeling the energy of who he *really* was, and went, "YUK!!!"

I call this phenomenon **"lust blindness"**—you meet someone whom you're *really, really, really* attracted to, and you mistake the intense sexual chemistry for compatibility. It's as if the lust blinds you to everything about the guy, and you convince yourself that he's the man of your dreams, when the truth is, you just have the hots for him. When you finally sleep with him, and the lust calms down, you suddenly see him as he really is . . . and you want to be sick. That's lust blindness!

REAL RULE #17 will help you protect yourself from lust blindness, from taking on a man's energy you didn't want, and from getting involved in relationships you shouldn't be in *by encouraging you to focus on developing the emotional intimacy, and not the physical.* It's like building the foundation of a house before you put up the walls and the ceiling. The foundation of a great relationship that is built to last a lifetime is *intimacy,* and not sex. Sure, sex is an important part of a marriage, but without the emotional commitment and compatibility, it's not enough to make a relationship work.

The basic rule is: **Postpone having sexual intercourse for as long as possible** (and I'm not talking about "holding out" for three weeks here!). I mean until you absolutely know that it's the right time, until you and your partner feel emotionally bonded, and until it feels totally unnatural to *not* make love. Here are some "requirements" I suggest you put into practice:

WHEN IS IT TIME TO BECOME SEXUALLY INTIMATE?

- *You should be **intellectually** intimate before you are sexually intimate.* That means, you should spend at least *twice as much time* talking and learning about one another as you do necking or fooling around. You should feel you can and do discuss anything and everything. You should have developed good, consistent communication about the relationship itself. You should know and like your partner's mind.

- *You should be **emotionally** intimate before you are sexually intimate.* That means you should feel a strong bond between your hearts, and share a closeness you don't experience with anyone else. You should have verbally shared deep feelings for one another, preferably feelings of "love." You should really love who this person is *on the inside,* not just his body or his good looks. You should want to make love to his inner being, not just his outer form.

- *You should really* like *the person.* I have a saying: DON'T SLEEP WITH SOMEONE YOU DON'T WANT TO BECOME LIKE. That means, you should *respect* him, his values, his character, the way he treats you and others, and the way he lives his life.

- *You should have discussed birth control, sexually transmitted diseases such as herpes and HIV, and know as much as possible about your partner's sexual history.* Both you and your partner should have been tested for the AIDS virus, and be aware of the results.

- *You should have agreed on what form of birth control you are going to use and made sure you'll be practicing safe sex.* You should have discussed pregnancy and your attitudes toward it, since it's always a possibility.

Each of us has different moral values that guide our decisions in life. You may believe that it is wrong to have sexual intercourse before marriage. Or you may think it's fine to have sex whenever and with whomever you wish. I'm not here to tell you what is right or wrong for you. What I *can* tell you is that following REAL RULE #17 will ensure that you don't end up just having sex with a partner, but truly making love; and that, whenever you do decide to share the beautiful experience of sexual union with a man, both of your hearts will be open, and therefore, *making love will do what its name suggests it's supposed to do: **make even more love between you.***

REAL RULE #18:

Don't Lower Yourself to Behaving Like a Sex Object

Let's be honest about something all women know, but will never admit out loud: **It's pathetically easy to use your sexuality to manipulate a man.** It doesn't even take any intelligence, style or, creativity. Wear a skin-tight, low-cut top, put on a really short skirt or form-fitting jeans you can hardly zip up, stick your cleavage under his nose, and according to the OLD RULES, you'll get a man's attention, right?

The REAL RULES say: SO WHAT?!! What's the big accomplishment if you get a man interested in you by waving your boobs in his face? That would be like offering a stray dog a big juicy bone and getting excited when he runs over to eat it, thinking, *"See, he really likes me!"* **Wake up, honey—it's not you he cares about, it's your meat!**

REAL RULE #18 says:

- **Don't lower yourself to behaving like a sex object in order to get a man to like you.**

- **Don't use sex to manipulate men unless you want to be seen only as a sex object.**

. . . AND . . .

- **If you do act and dress like a sex object, expect to be treated like one.**

Not behaving like a sex object means:

- **Don't bat your eyes and continually give a man suggestive looks.**
- **Don't stand too close to him or brush your body against his.**
- **Don't get drunk and act stupid.**
- **Don't act coy and teasing.**
- **Don't make suggestive remarks.**

I'm *not* saying that you shouldn't do these things with your boyfriend of six months (except, in my opinion, getting drunk and stupid). This REAL RULE is about not presenting yourself as a sex object in the beginning of a relationship when a man is forming his first impression of you.

Let's talk about clothes for a minute. There's nothing wrong in wearing clothes that make you feel beautiful, feminine, even sexy, when appropriate. And once you're in a serious relationship, it's fun to dress in a way that pleases both you and your partner. But remember—in the very beginning of a relationship, or before you even meet a guy, you are going to be judged by how you look on the outside.

And *based on how you dress, you'll attract different kinds of men.*

I know a woman who constantly complains that she can't find the right man, and only attracts jerks who "want one thing—namely, sex." If you took one look at her, you'd know in an instant what her problem is: *She dresses like a slut.* She makes herself appear to be some trashy babe with overteased, overbleached hair, clothes that are barely clinging to her body, and more makeup than a drag queen. Her physical presence gives off one message: I WANT YOU TO SCREW ME. Then she gets upset when men want to do just that.

Men are very visual creatures, and they don't do a lot of intellectual interpretation when it comes to what they see: **If you dress like a slut, a man will think you're a slut. If you dress like a classy woman, he'll think you're a classy woman. If you dress tastefully in a way that flatters you and reflects your own personal style, he'll think you're attractive *and* intelligent.**

Your outside appearance should reflect how you feel on the inside. *If you present an image of yourself that isn't the "real you," don't be surprised if you attract men who don't love you for who you really are.* There are men who are so afraid of intimacy and have such a self-esteem problem that they're looking for a woman who will be a good-looking accessory, rather than one with whom to have a meaningful relationship. So if you advertise yourself as an accessory, that's the kind of buyer you'll get.

Don't you want a man to love you for *who you are on the inside*, and *not just how you look on the outside*? **Then don't overemphasize the outside, or he'll never get past it.** If you dress in a way that puts all the attention on your body and your sexuality, it will be difficult for the right man to take you seriously in other ways. Besides, how can you ever be confident that he really loves you for your true self if you're catering to every visual fantasy he has?

Again, once you're in a balanced, loving relationship, it's fun to please your partner by wearing clothes he enjoys, but only if you feel comfortable doing it, and only if you know that he loves you just as much when you wear your sweats or oversized T-shirts!

The kind of man you want to marry, a man who will be a good husband and father, isn't out there looking for a woman who's a porno magazine fantasy. He's looking for a best friend, a loving companion, and someone he can be proud of. Remember: **the more you share your mind and your heart with a man, the more of you there is for him to fall in love with.**

In the end, what's truly sexy is *confidence, warmth, intelligence, and love.* When you show those parts of yourself to the *right* man, he will know you for the unique and special woman that you are, and he won't be able to resist you!!

REAL RULE #19:
Apply THE REAL RULES in Bed

Let's say you've followed THE REAL RULES to meet the right man, you've developed an emotionally and intellectually intimate relationship, and now you've both agreed that it's time to make love. DON'T FORGET ABOUT THE REAL RULES JUST BECAUSE YOU GET INTO BED WITH A GUY! In fact, practicing THE REAL RULES in bed is one of the best ways to create a passionate and fulfilling sex life.

Here's how you can apply some of the REAL RULES to your sexual relationship with a man:

REAL RULE #2: *Remember That Men Need as Much Love and Reassurance as You Do*

You know how nervous you get when you're anticipating those first few sexual encounters with someone you've fallen in love with? Well, don't forget that he's just as nervous as you are! THE REAL RULES remind you that no matter how wonderful you think this guy is, and how much you want him to love you, he's only human and has the same insecurities and needs that you have. Remembering this will help you to relax, to not worry so much about everything having to be perfect, and to let him into your heart.

REAL RULE #4: *Don't Play Games*

Games are all about deception, and there's no place for that in the bedroom. Some of the sexual games you *shouldn't* play if you're practicing THE REAL RULES are:

"Try to Guess How I'm Feeling"

"First I Want You, Then I Don't"

"No Matter What You Do, I'm Not Impressed"

"You're Not Getting Sex Until I See the Ring"

Don't use sex to manipulate a man into doing what you want him to do, or to convince him to continue to see you when he's already indicated he wants to break up, or to get even with him for something he did by seducing him and then acting as if he's a terrible lover—these are all games that aren't part of THE REAL RULES.

And needless to say, NEVER, NEVER fake an orgasm.

REAL RULE #5: *Be Yourself*

Don't try to become some kind of woman you think your partner wants in bed. Be yourself, because that's the only thing you can do really well anyway. That means, if you aren't into wild, adventurous sex, don't try to act that way. If you feel very emotional, and find yourself wanting to cry, don't hold back. If you are a little shy and inexperienced, don't pretend you've had sex hundreds of times. The more natural you are, the easier it will be for you and your partner to connect from the heart and really make love.

Be yourself also means *don't do things you're uncomfortable doing, even if it means jeopardizing the relationship.* If you aren't into kinky sex, and your boyfriend brings out the handcuffs and satin whip, let him know he'd better put them away fast. If your boyfriend wants to have sex three times a day and that's just too much for you, don't do it anyway and then resent him for it. You don't have to apologize for your preferences, or even explain them. But THE REAL RULES say you must honor them if you're going to be yourself.

REAL RULE #10: *Pay Attention to Warning Signs of Possible Problems*

Having sex with someone is a very revealing experience. You will learn things about a man when *you're in bed with him that you wouldn't learn in any other way.* Pay attention to any warning signs of possible problems such as:

- **Your partner is very controlling in bed**—he gives you instructions, tells you when to move, turns you this way and that, and dominates the whole experience. Men like this either feel out of control in their regular lives, or afraid of being controlled by a woman. Either way, you're involved with a control freak!

- **Your partner races to get sex over with**—he might secretly feel sex is dirty, and feels guilty enjoying it.

- **Your partner is an insensitive, selfish lover**—he may also be an insensitive, selfish person and you've just never noticed it before.

- **Your partner is a sexual performer**—he seems really into how good *he* is in bed, and you begin to feel it doesn't really matter who he is with, because it's about him. This guy is probably self-centered, narcissistic, and incapable of really loving anyone but himself.

- **Your partner is totally inexpressive**—if he's quiet as a mouse, hardly gives you any indication that he's enjoying himself, and you can't even tell that he came, you're with a guy who has a pretty hard time expressing his feelings, in or out of bed.

- **Your partner can't have sex without being high or intoxicated**—a man who can't have sex without getting stoned or drunk has an addiction, whether or not he acknowledges it. *If your partner needs to be high to enjoy sex, he has a real prob-*

lem. Either he should get help, or you should get out.

These are just a few of the warning signs to watch out for. There are dozens more. When in doubt, ask your girlfriends or guy friends what they think about your man's sexual behavior. They'll probably be able to interpret signs more accurately than you will, since they have no investment in the relationship.

REAL RULE #14: *Be Honest About Your Feelings*

THE REAL RULES are all about honest communication, not about guessing games. So when it comes to your sex life:

- *Tell your partner what you like and dislike*
- *Let him know how you feel*
- *Be emotionally open so he can be emotionally open*
- *Talk together when you're not in bed about your attitudes toward sex, your wants and your needs*
- *Educate him about your body. He doesn't have one like yours, so he won't know what to do with it as well as you do*

REAL RULE #16: *Be Emotionally Generous,* Not *Emotionally Stingy*

When you're in bed with the man you love, use words (and sounds!) to show your appreciation. Let him know what he's doing right. Let him know what feels good. Tell him how much you love what he's doing. Tell him how what he's doing makes you feel in your heart. Show him how much he turns you on. Show him how much you want to turn him on. Let your passion out!!

Have fun practicing THE REAL RULES in bed!!

Part 5

THE REAL RULES ABOUT GETTING A MAN TO MAKE A COMMITMENT

REAL RULE #20:
Make Sure Your Relationship Goes Through the Four Stages of Commitment

Have you ever been in a relationship, and everything is going along fine, until you bring up the topic of "commitment"?

Do you ever worry that, even though you don't want to put pressure on a man to commit, if you don't, he'll never ask you to marry him?

When your boyfriend says he loves you, but he's just not ready to "make a commitment," what does he mean?

I don't think there's any one word in our language that can cause more tension between men and women than *the "C" word:* **COMMITMENT.** We fight over it, worry about it, and sometimes break up because of it. It brings out our worst stereotypes about the opposite sex: Men think the purpose of a woman's life is to try and trap a guy into making a commitment; women think men are commitment-phobic, and will only give in and finally pop the question under extreme duress.

After working with thousands of couples over many years, I've come to the conclusion that a lot of our problems with commitment could be avoided, if we understood REAL RULE #20—**that making a commitment isn't about making a decision one day to marry someone. There are actually *four stages of commitment* every relationship should go through, and therefore, four decisions each couple makes over time.**

If you're like most people, you unconsciously equate the word "commitment" with the word "marriage." For instance, let's say you meet a guy, and really like him. You date each other for about six months, and all of a sudden, start feeling like you need a "commitment" to solidify the relationship. So you ask yourself *"Do I want to get engaged and marry this person?"* If it's too soon to be able to answer that question, which it probably is, you become confused and wonder *"What do I do now? Does my lack of certainty mean I should break up with him?"*

The answer is: NO. What's happening is that you are ready for a new level of commitment—just not the commitment of marriage. But if you don't understand REAL RULE #20, you won't know what that next level of commitment is, and could actually sabotage a perfectly wonderful relationship.

Imagine for a minute that you decide to talk about this issue with your boyfriend You say, **"Honey, I feel like I need more of a commitment from you."** What's the first thing he thinks? **You got it . . . he thinks you want him to propose!**

He says to himself: *"Gosh, I love her and everything, but I'm definitely not ready to get married."* So he may respond to you by saying, *"Look, I can't make a commitment right now."* You hear this and burst into tears, concluding, "He doesn't love me. He's not serious about us." And maybe, you even break up with him, telling your girlfriends that he just didn't want a committed relationship.

So there you both are, miserable, missing each other, and *totally misunderstanding what happened.* The truth is, you probably wanted the same thing—A DEEPER LEVEL OF COMMITMENT, BUT NOT MARRIAGE QUITE YET. However, without knowing the levels of commitment, you couldn't even talk clearly with each other about what you needed.

Here is a description of the four levels of commitment a relationship passes through as it grows. I think you'll find them helpful in understanding your own relationships and knowing when it's time to move on to the next level.

COMMITMENT LEVEL #1: Commitment to Be Sexually and Emotionally Monogamous

Time: 0 to three months

If you are single and dating, you will probably spend some time getting to know a new partner, and figuring out if you want to keep seeing him. At some point, *within weeks and certainly by a few months*, you will need some kind of commitment in order to go forward. This should be a commit-

ment to be sexually and emotionally monoga-
mous. I call this *A New Relationship.*

Here are **agreements** you and your partner
should make with one another when you enter
into a LEVEL ONE COMMITMENT:

1. You and your partner agree that this is your
   one and only intimate relationship, and
   commit to putting your time and energy into
   sharing with one another and no one else.
2. Your and your partner agree that you are each
   other's **only sexual partners** ("sex" meaning
   everything from kissing to intercourse—whatever level you are participating in).

If a man refuses to make a Level One Commitment very soon into the relationship, I urge you to
say good-bye right then and there. **Your relationship will not be able to grow without monog-
amy, and if your partner doesn't respect and
value you enough to offer you that commitment,
he's not worth waiting for.**

COMMITMENT LEVEL #2: Commitment to Work Toward a Partnership

Time: Three to six months

Once you and your partner are monogamously
dating and make it to three or four months, your

relationship will probably become *"serious." You consider yourself "in love"—you're officially a couple.* **This is a crucial stage of a relationship, during which you are going to become more emotionally involved. Therefore, you want to be sure you're making the right decision before making yourself even more vulnerable.** You should spend your time deepening your knowledge of one another and testing your compatibility by practicing THE REAL RULES. I call this stage *A Developing Relationship*

When you feel:

- Your relationship is getting better and better
- You are sharing most aspects of your time and life together
- You are starting to think as a "we,"

. . . then you are ready for a **Level Two Commitment: Working Toward a Partnership.**

Here are **agreements** you and your partner should make with one another when you enter into a LEVEL TWO COMMITMENT:

- You and your partner agree that **your relationship is special and worth nurturing.**
- You and your partner agree that your relationship has **the *potential* to be a lasting partnership.**

- You and your partner agree to work together through honestly communicating feelings, looking at your own blocks to intimacy, and learning to understand one another **in order to create that potential lasting partnership.**

It's during this Developing Stage of relationships that a lot of us make the mistake of not getting a Level Two Commitment. You *assume* your partner sees a possible future with you—otherwise, why would he be saying he loves you and spending all that time with you. You don't actually talk about your assumptions, and one day months later, your heart gets broken when you bring up marriage or something comparable, and he responds by saying *"I never said we would have a future together. I don't love you that way."*

DON'T STAY IN A DEVELOPING RELATIONSHIP FOR MORE THAN FOUR TO SIX MONTHS WITHOUT GETTING A LEVEL TWO COMMITMENT.

COMMITMENT LEVEL #3: Commitment to Spend Your Future Together

Time: Six months to however long you need

Once you've agreed to work on creating a partnership together, you could spend anywhere from

six months to several years building that partnership, depending on how old you both are and the
circumstances surrounding your relationship. **My
advice is the younger you are, the more time you
should spend before agreeing to a Level Three
Commitment.** If you are in your early twenties, I
don't suggest you make a Level Three Commitment after knowing a guy for only six months. To
be honest, you probably need several years of
learning relationship skills and emotional matu-
rity to give your love a strong foundation. If you
are in your thirties, have had serious relationships,
and are very clear about who you are and what
you want, you may not need (or want to spend)
this much time developing a partnership, and may
be ready to commit to a future together within the
first year. Each couple's case will be different.

You are ready to make a Level Three Commitment when:

- You have created a strong and healthy partnership that is functioning well almost all of
  the time
- You feel sure that you want to spend your future together, if not the rest of your life
- You have no desire to investigate anyone else
  as a possible partner
- You feel totally loved and appreciated by your
  partner almost all of the time

Here are **agreements** you and your partner should make with one another when you enter into a LEVEL THREE COMMITMENT:

- You and your partner agree that **you want to spend your future together.**
- You and your partner agree to **formalize your commitment** by either:
  - becoming engaged to be married
  - *planning* on becoming engaged as soon as you can
  - deciding to live together
- You and your partner agree to continue working on yourselves and the relationship in order to **eliminate any remaining doubts or obstacles to a successful lifetime commitment.**

You've probably noticed that a Level Three Commitment is an agreement to spend the foreseeable future together, but not the indefinite future, as in forever. *You know you want to spend your life together, but for various reasons, you aren't totally ready to formalize that desire and get married now. (That would be a Level Four Commitment.)*

Making a Level Three Commitment will look different from couple to couple, depending on how traditional or nontraditional your values are, and on the circumstances surrounding your relationship. If you feel strongly about living with a man during your Level Three Commitment but want the formal structure of marriage somewhere down the road, you need to discuss this *before* you actually move in together in order to avoid any misunderstandings. *You may want to come up with a time projection, nine months or a year after moving in together, for instance, at which point you **will reevaluate your relationship and decide whether or not you feel ready to marry.***

COMMITMENT LEVEL #4: Commitment to Spend the Rest of Your Lives Together

This is what most of us think of when we use the word "commitment"—marriage. You are ready for a Level Four Commitment when:

- You've had a Level Three Commitment for some time (engaged, living together, etc.) and *have worked through whatever circumstantial obstacles or emotional issues were in your way.*
- You have total trust and faith in your relationship and its ability to continue to grow as well as survive whatever adversity it faces.
- You feel excited about exploring deeper levels of love, intimacy, and surrender with your partner.
- You are sure that you and your partner have enough compatibility to be "right" for each other.

Here are **agreements** you and your partner should make with one another when you enter into a LEVEL FOUR COMMITMENT:

- You and your partner agree that you want to spend the rest of your lives together.
- You and your partner agree that as lifelong mates, your relationship becomes your creation, your "child," **and you will cherish, protect, and nurture that child called your partnership.**
- You and your partner agree to any other commitments you both feel are important to inaugurate your new level of oneness.

For most people, a Level Four Commitment is expressed by becoming legally married. For others who are less traditional, it may be expressed in a nonlegal ceremony, or in another private way in which they consecrate their relationship. Whatever form it takes, a Level Four Commitment is the highest form of commitment you can make to another person.

Now that you've learned about these four kinds of commitments, I hope you see why saying to a man "I need a commitment" can not only be confusing, but inaccurate. He may think you want to get married, and you may just want to make sure he isn't sleeping with anyone else!

How do you bring up these commitments and the agreements you want from your boyfriend? Remember *REAL RULE #14: Be honest about your feelings.* Just say what you want to say. You might begin by asking him what he needs from you to continue in the relationship, and then mention what you need from him. Even better, pull out a copy of THE REAL RULES and show him this section, and ask him what he thinks? What if he disagrees with everything, or refuses to discuss it? A WARNING SIGN!!! After all, if you can't even talk about this stuff, you shouldn't be together in the first place, and certainly shouldn't become engaged.

I think that when you bring up the subject of levels of commitment vs. the "big commitment," you'll discover a secret about REAL RULE #20: **MEN LOVE IT!!** When you share this kind of specific information with your partner, he'll probably give a huge sigh of relief, and think *"What a smart and articulate woman!"* Instead of feeling pressured to make a *premature* commitment to marriage, your boyfriend can now commit one step at a time, understand your needs, make you happy, and feel confident that, when he does ask you to marry him, you'll both be totally ready.

REAL RULE #21:
Emotional Commitments Are More Valuable Than an Engagement Ring

THE OLD RULES believe that the purpose of your relationship with a man, from the moment you meet him, is to get him to ask you to marry him, and offer you a beautiful engagement ring. THE REAL RULES SAY: If that's all a man offers you when he proposes, you're going to get ripped off. WHY? **Because it's not the ring, or the proposal, that will make your relationship last a lifetime—it's the emotional commitments a man offers you from his heart.**

Here's the problem: we often get so caught up in "waiting" for the proposal and the ring that we forget to look for the emotional commitments that are the real foundation of a great marriage. I hear stories like the following one all the time . . .

A woman has been going out with a guy for a year or two; her friends and family keep asking her when she and her boyfriend are getting married; her sister just got engaged; and soon, all she can think about is: "Will he propose on my birthday? Will he propose on Christmas Day? Will he propose after he graduates?" The proposal becomes her goal.

What is this woman doing wrong? *She's focusing on*

the wrong thing, the proposal, and not on the most impor-tant thing—how emotionally committed her boyfriend is to talk about his feelings, fulfill her needs, and work with her to create a healthy relationship.

Finally one day, he does ask her to marry him, and gives her a beautiful diamond ring. She did it! She got him to propose! Her friends and family are ec-static, and for months, she's walking on air! "Let's see the ring!" everyone asks, and each time she proudly displays it, she thinks to herself, "I'm so happy."

But at some point, either during the engagement, or worse, after they're married, she begins to realize that the relationship has some serious problems. Her husband is putting all of his time into his career, and none into the marriage. He refuses to talk about any-thing she's unhappy with, and answers her com-plaints with the comment, "That's just the way I am."

Did these problems mysteriously manifest after the wedding? Did her husband change so much from when they were engaged? *NO! These issues were there all along, but his wife was too busy looking for signs that he might propose, rather than looking for signs that he was truly emotionally committed.*

If she'd been using THE REAL RULES, and had been honest with herself, this woman would have noticed that although her man offered her a ring, he didn't ever offer to talk about their problems, make her more of a priority, or work on his own issues.

This story could happen to you—unless you remember **REAL RULE #21: Emotional commitments are much more valuable than an engagement ring.**

Emotional commitments are promises you and your partner make to one another about how you each plan to grow as an individual and a couple. They are things you should talk about over and over again *BEFORE* you get married, preferably before you even get engaged. Here are four basic emotional commitments I suggest you look for from the man you want to spend your life with.

1. I am committed to learning everything I can about being a better person and a better mate.

That means, I will actively work on improving myself and getting rid of any of my unhealthy emotional habits so I can be a loving, giving partner.

2. I am committed to learning how to love you as much as you deserve to be loved.

That means, I will work hard to express my love through words and through affection, and to fulfill your needs.

3. I am committed to doing whatever it takes to make our relationship work.

That means, when we have problems, I will be open to discussing them, and using books, tapes, counseling, or any other tools available to help our marriage.

4. I am committed to staying emotionally open in our relationship.

That means, I will communicate my feelings to you, let you know what's going on inside of me, and reach out, rather than push you away.

In many ways, these four commitments mean much more than your man saying, "I'm committed to marrying you." I believe strongly that it's not a wedding ceremony or a license that creates true commitment. Marriage is not a piece of paper. It's not wearing a ring or collecting photo albums of your vacations. It's not saying how many years you've lived in the same house. Instead:

MARRIAGE IS THE WAY YOU LOVE, HONOR, AND RESPECT YOUR PARTNER DAY BY DAY AS AN EXPRESSION OF YOUR EMOTIONAL COMMITMENT TO ONE ANOTHER.

You aren't married because you had a big party, or because you sent in twenty-five dollars to the county, or because everyone thinks you are. *You are truly married when you and your partner resonate together mentally, emotionally, physically, and spiritually.* **It is a choice you make, not just on one special day, but over and over again, and that choice is reflected in the emotional commitments you practice in each moment.**

I find so many young couples who live with the dangerous misconception: "Once we're married, everything will be great." Your wedding ceremony or big party or one carat ring isn't going to help you create a happy marriage—*but your emotional commitments will.*

I love the beautiful ring my husband gave me when he asked me to marry him. But compared to the emotional promises he made and kept, that ring means nothing. It's those commitments he offered me that made me sure I was marrying the right man, and that have allowed our marriage to grow in love, respect, and joy every day.

REAL RULE #22:
Never Pressure a Man Into Making a Commitment

There comes a point in many women's lives when, in spite of how much we think we've worked on our self-esteem and self-respect, in spite of our most honorable and good intentions, and in spite of the fact that we know better, **we put the pressure on a man we love to make a commitment.** Some of us are subtle about it (or so we think!), hoping somehow that our discreet references will put ideas into our sweetheart's head. We start mentioning every friend, cousin, neighbor, or distant acquaintance who just got engaged, always with great longing in our voice, and followed by a heavy pause. We insert the word "future" into conversations every chance we can get: *"I told my boss I wasn't sure if I could go to the convention next year because I didn't know what might be happening in my FUTURE"* (hint, hint).

Some of us become mysteriously depressed and distant in the presence of our man. We sigh a lot, gaze off into the distance with forlorn looks on our faces, and when our boyfriend tell us he loves us, but doesn't say anything further, we look sad and wistful, as if he's just said something upsetting. When he asks us what's wrong, we sigh even more deeply and respond, *"Oh, nothing . . . really,"* as we give him a look that's supposed to make him feel he's done something awful (although naturally, he has *no idea* what it could be).

These behaviors usually have little or no effect on our boyfriends, since most men aren't trained to interpret these esoteric symptoms, and probably conclude that we have an extended case of PMS!

Some women (not YOU, of course!) who are even more desperate and misguided than others actually resort to outright manipulation and trickery using the OLD RULES. When a woman like this feels a proposal is overdue, she threatens to start seeing other men, takes long vacations without her boyfriend, doesn't answer his phone calls, or moves to another city, hoping that when he thinks he can't have her, he'll be pushed over the edge and will finally ask her to marry him.

Do these deceptive tactics work? Let's put it this way: sometimes, as we've seen, the WRONG MEN *will* go after women who play games; they may even propose. **But is this kind of proposal worth anything when it's been practically forced out of the guy?** Not to me, it isn't, and it shouldn't be worth anything to you either.

There is no joy in trapping a man into making a commitment, or pressuring him into proposing, any more than there's joy in spending money you stole, rather than money you earned.

What we're talking about here is the difference between *conquest*, an OLD RULES concept, *and commit-*

ment, a REAL RULES concept. Conquest means that you manipulate and pressure a guy into marrying you, and you conclude that you've "won" the power struggle between your desire to get married and his desire to be free. He was your prey and you finally trapped him. **Commitment, on the other hand, is something you can't "capture" from someone—it has to be given freely, and that's why it is so precious.** When a man makes a commitment to you from his heart, he is offering you a great gift of love, and honoring you as his soulmate.

REAL RULE #22 says: **Never pressure a man into making a commitment.** Follow all the other REAL RULES by sharing your feelings honestly, asking questions, being yourself, and going through the four levels of commitment. If you come to a point in the relationship where you need more of a commitment than he's willing to give, and you've talked openly about it with one another, then it's time to move on so you can find the right person for you. It's NOT the time to try to manipulate that commitment out of him. How much would that kind of commitment be worth? *How secure could you feel marrying someone knowing that you "tricked" him into it?*

Here's another way to think about it by reversing the situation. **Let's say your new boyfriend of three weeks really wants to have sex with you, but you don't feel ready to make love yet.** He decides to follow a man's version of THE OLD RULES to get you into bed. He starts acting cold and distant, and looking lustfully at other women in front of you; he nonchalantly mentions that he just had lunch with his ex-lover, the gorgeous nymphomaniac model with the perfect body (who wants him back, by the way); and informs you that he's planning a trip to Club Med in Tahiti—alone.

"Oh no," you think to yourself, "I'm losing him. Maybe I should just go ahead and sleep with him now so he doesn't turn to someone else." And so even though you aren't ready, even though it's against your principles, you have sex with him—out of fear.

Does this story make your stomach turn? Does it make you angry to think about how easily women give in to sexual pressure from guys, just because we don't want to feel rejected? Does it make you want to say, "Men like that are scum?" Probably . . . but ask yourself: How different is this man's behavior from a woman who manipulates her boyfriend into proposing? No different at all . . .

I believe that if a man is meant to be yours, you can never lose him, and if he's not, you can never have him anyway, no matter how hard you try. **When you're in the *right relationship*, with the *right man*, you will both know, at the *right time*, that you are meant to spend the rest of your life together.** And that magical moment will be worth waiting for.

Part 6

HOW TO LIVE YOUR LIFE WITH THE REAL RULES

REAL RULE #23:
Be Patient as You Switch From the Old Rules to the Real Rules

Now you're ready for the exciting part: Beginning to put the REAL RULES into practice in your relationships with men. If you've been following some of the OLD RULES, you may *want* to change and start applying the REAL RULES in your relationships with men, but not be quite certain how to go about it. Or, maybe you've tried a REAL RULE or two already, and weren't sure if you were doing it right.

It's perfectly natural to feel that way. After all, you may be used to playing games, or editing certain parts of yourself you don't think a man will like, not asking for what you want, or focusing so much on getting him to like *you*, that you don't stop and ask yourself how much you really like who *he* is. *If this is how you're used to thinking and behaving, even part of the time, it's going to feel a little strange in the beginning doing exactly the opposite of what is familiar to you.*

Here's something important to remember: **Just because something feels uncomfortable or awkward at first *doesn't* mean it's not good for you.** Think back to the first time you rode a bike, or drove a car, or learned to dance, or kissed a boy. Do you remember how nervous you were, how awkward you felt? Well, fortunately, you didn't interpret your discomfort as a sign that you should never do that activity again. You persevered, and before long, riding the bike or driving or dancing or kissing felt as natural as they had previously felt unnatural.

The same is true for THE REAL RULES. You may go through a brief transition period between OLD RULES behavior and REAL RULES behavior when you feel a little unsure of yourself. **After all, maybe for the first time, you're letting your real personality shine, and totally being yourself with a man.** The experience of being calm, confident, and natural around men may be so unusual for you that, at first, it might feel weird. *"How can this be a date?"* you may wonder, *"I'm so relaxed!"* CONGRATULATIONS— you're practicing THE REAL RULES!

Here's an easy-to-remember four-step formula for switching from THE OLD RULES to THE REAL RULES:

THE REAL RULES FORMULA

1. Notice when you're uncomfortable around a man or in a relationship.

2. Ask yourself, "What OLD RULE behavior am I practicing that's making me uncomfortable?"

3. Then ask yourself, "What REAL RULE can I put into practice right now that will bring me back to center?"

4. Finally, put that REAL RULE into practice.

Let's look at an example of how this works: You read this book, and soon after you go out on a date with a new guy. As you're sitting in the restaurant, you notice that you're beginning to feel very uncomfortable. You hear yourself making mindless chatter about the weather, what movies you like, and other topics you couldn't care less about. *"This isn't going well—I sound like a stupid idiot,"* you worry.

Then, you remember THE REAL RULES Formula. *"Aha—I'm noticing I'm uncomfortable. That's step one"* you remind yourself. Okay, what's step two? **Ask yourself what OLD RULE behavior you're practicing that's making you feel awkward.** *"Well, I'm trying to keep things light and easy, I'm editing a lot of what I'm thinking, and I'm not showing my real personality."*

Great! You've just pinpointed exactly why you feel so awkward—*you're not being yourself.* No wonder you aren't having a good time. Now what? Step three: **Ask yourself, "What REAL RULE can I put into practice right now that will bring me back to center?"**

"Well, I have a few to choose from: I could ask him questions to find out more about him. I could be honest

about my feelings. I could show my mind and be more of who I really am!"

Excellent! So now it's time for step four: **put THE REAL RULE into practice.** And so you do:

"Jim, I have to confess I'm a little nervous tonight— I've heard so many great things about you from your brother that he made you sound practically perfect!" **(Be Honest About Your Feelings, #14)** . . . OR:

"You mentioned that you just moved to New York from Ohio. Has the transition been difficult? I know it was for me when I moved here from North Carolina after college." **(Ask Questions, #7)** . . . OR

"Something you just said about your nephew's birthday party reminded me of this great book I just read about traditional Native American rituals. Do you know when a young boy turned a certain age, he was sent off for three days on a vision quest to seek his own spirit guides and have mystical experiences? That sounds kind of cool, don't you think?" **(Show Your Mind, #15)**

There, it's that simple. When you follow the REAL RULES FORMULA, you'll start catching yourself doing or saying what isn't authentically YOU, and be able to make a new, healthy choice by practicing a REAL RULE.

Breaking old habits doesn't happen overnight—it takes time. Whether it's smoking, overeating, biting your nails, procrastinating, following old, outdated rules about how to act with men, or any other behavior that isn't good for you, making positive changes is a step-by-step process that requires a lot of patience and self-love. So be proud of yourself for deciding to make a change, and rediscover the powerful and lovable woman you truly are. *And don't pressure yourself to do it all perfectly overnight.*

Before you know it, you won't even have to think about how you're acting or coming across with men anymore—**you'll always be comfortable expressing your true personality, sharing your thoughts and feelings, and letting your beautiful and unique inner self shine!!** And that will give the *right man* a chance to get to know the *real you* and fall in love!

REAL RULE #24:
Protect Yourself With Your Head, Not Your Heart

At this point in the book, you may be thinking to yourself, *"Well, this all sounds wonderful, but what if I follow THE REAL RULES and get hurt in a relationship anyway? What if I'm myself, and a man rejects me? What if I ask questions and he calls me 'controlling'? What if I let him know how I feel, and he gets scared and leaves?"*

My answer is: **If it happens, move on. Remember—the wrong men will automatically eliminate themselves from your love life when you practice THE REAL RULES.**

You don't need every man in the world to love you. You only need *one man* in the world to love you. **Using THE REAL RULES to quickly find out that the wrong man isn't interested in you doesn't mean you've failed. On the contrary, it means you've been** *successful:* **one more incompatible partner eliminated, one more waste-of-time relationship avoided, one step closer to finding the right man.**

Let's be honest. None of us like being rejected, even by people we can't stand! It hurts when anyone doesn't think you're beautiful, brilliant, and desirable—that's called your *ego*. But you can't avoid some degree of pain in life and in love. It's part of being human. Even when you're happily married, if your husband gets upset with you about something, it's going to hurt a little until you kiss and make up.

Women who are driven by a chronic fear of pain and rejection, and who decide to avoid pain at all costs become cold, protected, and unreachable. *Their fear puts up walls around their heart that no one can get past*, and when a potentially right man comes along, he sees her walls, decides it's just too much work to break them down, and moves on to someone else.

The OLD RULES advise you to *protect yourself with your heart*, by not showing your feelings, remaining mysterious and unreachable, and letting the man be the one who is vulnerable and takes all the risks. **Not only will these behaviors** *fail to protect you from pain*—**they will ultimately** *lead* **to pain, as you manipulate your way into marriage with a man who doesn't know or love the real you, and only responds to game-playing.**

REAL RULE #24 says: **Protect yourself with your head, not your heart. In other words:**

DON'T CLOSE YOUR HEART— INSTEAD, BE SMART.

Being smart means using your intelligence and THE REAL RULES to:

- Stay away from men who don't like THE REAL RULES (#3)

- Be yourself (#5)
- Ask questions before you get too involved (#7)
- Don't date men who aren't completely available (#8)
- Look for a man with good character (#9)
- Pay attention to warning signs of possible problems (#10)
- Don't fall in love with a man's potential (#13)
- Be honest about your feelings (#14)
- Show your mind (#15)
- Wait until you're emotionally intimate before becoming sexually intimate (#17)
- Don't lower yourself to behaving like a sex object (#18) . . . AND,
- Make sure your relationship goes through the four stages of commitment (#20)

When you use your head to follow these REAL RULES with men, you will avoid a tremendous amount of potential pain and heartache, and will feel confident that you won't end up in the wrong relationship with the wrong person.

Your ability to feel deeply is your greatest gift. Don't shut off your heart out of fear. Instead, use THE REAL RULES to tap into your own inner power and natural wisdom, and follow their voices until they lead you to your true love.

REAL RULE #25:
Use THE REAL RULES With Everyone in Your Life

Have you guessed the secret behind THE REAL RULES yet? I'll give you a hint—THE REAL RULES are much more than suggestions for finding the right man, or advice for creating a fulfilling relationship with your soulmate. They're not even rules about men at all.

Here's the truth about THE REAL RULES: **They're THE REAL RULES about life.** *They're based on spiritual and philosophical principles that don't just apply to intimate relationships, but to your relationships with everyone, including your family, your friends, the people you work with, even people you hardly know.*

This is what's so exciting about THE REAL RULES. Once you understand them, you can use them in all kinds of situations with all kinds of people. **In fact, you don't even have to be in an intimate relationship right now to start practicing THE REAL RULES.** It's true—you don't even need a man to use THE REAL RULES. You can begin to apply them to how you relate to the other people in your life, so that when the right man comes along, you'll already be comfortable using THE REAL RULES.

See, for every problem you've had in a relationship with a man, I'll bet you've had just as many problems in your relationships with friends, family, coworkers, employees, etc. That's because most of us are making the same mistakes with these people that we make with our lovers. *The same OLD RULES that don't work in intimate relationships don't work in any relationships,* yet many of us unknowingly use these OLD rules in all areas of our life.

For instance, have you ever ended up in a job you couldn't stand? Maybe you were so focused on getting hired that you didn't stop to ask enough questions about the job, the working environment, the philosophy of the company, so you could determine whether or not this job was right for you! Sound familiar? It's just what we do when we're desperate for a relationship and don't ask the guy enough questions before getting involved (REAL RULE #7)

Perhaps you have a girlfriend who's driving you crazy because she keeps coming to you complaining about her life. And the truth is, her life is a mess. She's always getting into destructive relationships with men who treat her like dirt, always drinking too much, getting fired from jobs, and creating one drama after another.

When you think back, you knew when you first met her that she had problems, but . . . you ignored them, and hoped that somehow, you could "help her" get her life together. *Can you see what REAL RULES you ignored here? REAL RULE #10. Pay attention to warning signs, and #13, don't fall in love with someone's potential.*

On the next few pages are a few of the REAL RULES reworded to apply to *all* of your relationships.

THE REAL RULES FOR LIFE

REAL RULE #1: *Treat People the Way You Want Them to Treat You*

If this was the only REAL RULE you followed in life, you'd be doing pretty well. It's really simple: if you don't like it when people lie to you, don't lie to them. If you don't like it when people gossip about you, don't gossip about them. If you don't like it when people don't give you a chance to explain yourself, don't tune them out when they're trying to explain themselves.

One way to remember this life rule is to think about the law of *karma*—that everything you do comes back to you. *Before you do something, ask yourself, "Am I willing to receive back the consequences of this action?"* If the answer is no, then don't do it!

REAL RULE #2: Remember That Everyone Needs as Much Love and Reassurance as You Do

Inside each person you meet is the same need for love, approval, and validation. Sure, some people have a really twisted way of getting those things, but most people do respond well if you *look past the personality they try to show you on the outside, and see the vulnerable human being on the inside.*

Remembering that the salesperson who's acting

like a jerk probably isn't getting a lot of love in his life, or that the guy who just tried to take credit for your work project probably feels totally inadequate, will help you to not overreact to life's inevitable disappointments. You may still be upset, but at least you won't lower yourself to the other person's level by acting just as badly.

Don't forget—everyone's just as scared as you are of not being loved.

REAL RULE #4: *Don't Play Games*

Deception and manipulation may temporarily work to get you certain results in your personal or professional life, *but they ultimately destroy your integrity and your character*. Be direct, be fair, and don't play games. You're better than that.

REAL RULE #5: *Be Yourself*

This rule always works in every situation, regardless of the apparent outcome or other people's reactions, *because you can't ever be good at being someone other than who you really are anyway*.

REAL RULE #6: *If You Like Someone, Let Him Know*

That means, your friends, your relatives, your neighbors, your bus driver, your waitress, your teacher, your salesperson, your aerobics instructor, your dogs and cats—everyone. And don't think they already know how you feel and don't need to hear it—they do!!

REAL RULE #7: *Ask Questions Before You Get Too Involved*

Before you rent an apartment, before you hire someone, before you go to a new restaurant, before you book a hotel, before you agree to help someone with a project, before you let someone cut your hair, before you buy an appliance, before you do anything important, ask questions!!! The majority of everyday problems we face in our lives could be avoided if we asked more questions (and actually listened to the answers!).

REAL RULE #9: *Surround Yourself With People Who Have Good Character*

Don't just choose friends, roommates, business partners, traveling companions, employees based on *convenience.* Surround yourself with people who have good character and you'll have a lot less unhappiness in your life.

REAL RULE #10: *Pay Attention to Warning Signs of Possible Problems*

Pay attention to your body, your car, your finances, your moods, what people say and don't say to you, how people treat you, *and especially, pay attention to the things you're uncomfortable paying attention to.* The universe is always giving us an abundance of messages. It's when we don't pay attention to them that we get in the most trouble.

REAL RULE #11: *Judge People by the Size of Their Hearts and Not by Anything Else*

None of the following things matter: how much money someone has, how important or flashy their job is, how attractive they are, how successful they've become, who they know, how many people know them, what their body looks like, what they wear, what they own, their sexual preference, or the color of their skin. *What does matter is what's inside a person's heart.* If you're going to be impressed by anything, be impressed by how good and loving a person is.

REAL RULE #14: *Be Honest About Your Feelings*

The alternative never works in the long run, so why even try it?

REAL RULE #15: *Show Your Most Attractive Feature—Your Mind*

No one has one like yours, so yours is the best one of its kind in the whole world. *Show it off!*

REAL RULE #16: *Be Emotionally Generous,* **Not** *Emotionally Stingy*

The more love you share with others, the more love you will feel in your own heart, because when love is flowing out you are its first beneficiary. *You never lose by loving, so share your love with everyone and everything through your smiles, your words, your actions, and your thoughts.* Don't stop at people—let your love touch animals, trees, flowers, clouds, and all of nature's miracles.

Wouldn't it be wonderful if everyone you knew and everyone you didn't know were all practicing THE REAL RULES at the same time . . . ?

CONCLUSION

When I sat down to write THE REAL RULES, I was under a lot of pressure—I had much less time than I usually do to complete a manuscript, and wondered if I could actually meet the deadline. But even though it seemed like an almost impossible task, I felt that I *had* to write this book, that I was *meant* to write it, and that somehow, it would get finished on time. I locked myself in my office, turned on the computer, and began.

My husband has lived with me through the writing of six books, and he's very familiar with the predictable emotions I go through when giving birth to a new one, from excitement, frustration, impatience, self-doubt, breakthrough, and back to excitement, over and over again.

One evening about four days into my writing, I was sitting at the computer wondering how I was ever going to get this book done. I looked the way I always look when I'm in "book labor"—I was wearing my baggiest, raggiest sweat suit; I hadn't washed my hair in three days; and I still had on my fuzzy bedroom slippers from that morning.

Suddenly, there was a knock at my office door, and in walked my husband, Jeffrey, whom I hadn't seen all day. He was carrying an enormous bouquet of beautiful, exotic flowers in one hand and a cup of my favorite coffee in the other. *"I brought you some things to help you write,"* he said with a smile on his face. *"I thought the flowers would fill your office with their great fragrance, and the coffee would keep you awake!"*

He bent down to give me a kiss, as if he didn't even notice my greasy hair or my frumpy clothes, and then he put an envelope that contained a card in front of me. *"Read it now,"* he suggested. *"I'm hoping it will inspire you."* And so I opened it and read:

Dear Sweetheart:

Thank you for working so hard, and for standing up for what's right. If you were one of the "OLD RULES" girls, I would not only *not* have married you, I wouldn't have even been your friend! In fact, not only would I not have been your friend, I wouldn't have had anything to do with you! In fact, not only would I not have had anything to do with you, *I would have run the other way!!!*

Thank you for being a REAL woman with REAL brains and a REALLY BIG HEART. Thank you for being completely YOU. I adore you.

Go get 'em!!!!

Jeffrey

Tears poured down my face as I read these precious words from my wonderful husband, the husband whom I'd finally found only after many painful years of following the wrong rules and choosing the wrong men, the husband who was the first man I'd ever been totally open, totally honest, and totally myself with, the husband who loved me just the way I was sitting there in that moment, the husband who reassured me, over and over again, that *I didn't have to be anything or anyone but myself to get his love.*

Suddenly, I realized that this moment in my marriage was exactly what THE REAL RULES was about—**a moment in which I could experience the exquisite freedom of knowing that I was being completely loved by being *myself!*** My husband wasn't bringing me flowers because I'd been acting distant, or because I'd been behaving coldly to "keep him on his toes." He didn't write me the wonderful card because I was pretending to be busy so he'd chase after me. No, his thoughtfulness and his caring were both an expression of his *love and respect* for me as a woman, as his friend, and as his wife.

This was love that wasn't dependent on how I looked, how interested I kept him, or how many times I let him take the lead. **That's because this was love that was *real*.**

I want you to have this same experience. I want you to know how it feels to have a man love you for *just being yourself*. I want you to know how it feels to *not have to do anything to earn his love*. I want you to know how it feels to experience love that is *real*.

You don't deserve anything less than this . . .

I wrote this book for you, with love and respect for who you really are. Please pass its message on to the women you love and respect, and the women you'd like to love and respect. And please pass its message on to the men you know and the men you meet, so they can learn to love and respect us.

Thank you from the bottom of my heart.

Barbara